First Published in Nigeria by
MayThird Publishing

Editors: Hameedah Kehinde
Segilola Sunmola
Cover Design: Aaishah Abd-ur-Razaaq
Book Design: Aaishah Abd-ur-Razaaq

www.aishahadams.com
me@aishahadams.com

Foreword

THE LAST CALL is a well captured book about death written
by Aishah Adams. The book is her reflection and thoughts about
death. The integration of her personal life experiences and the
experiences of her close allies make the book more relatable.
Furthermore, the hadith of the prophet (sallallaahu alayhi
wassalam) that borders around death and Quranic quotations
about the same topic make the book a spiritual reflection.

The book contains five chapters. Chapter one discusses life as a
gift. Life is a gift. No human being owns his own life. As such,
life is a gift that has to be cherished. How do you cherish life?
The only way is to use it wisely in the worship of Allah. And
never forget that death is certain. A reality that every human will
come to terms with.

In chapter two of the book, the writer is blunt with the reality.
The reality of death, which we all shy away from discussing.
Death is coming for us all, whether we like it or not. The most
important thing is to accept this reality and prepare for death by
acquiring a lot of good deeds which we can be remembered for.

Our living and death must be for the sake of Allah. Which is
why chapter three of this book discusses preparation for death.
How do we prepare for death? Let's remember death as much as
we can. This will modify our actions in the way of Allah. He
who remembers death often is regarded as a thoughtful person.
A thoughtful person will always be mindful of his deeds. How
do you plan your exit? The answer is the way you live? He who
wants to end well must live well. Like the popular saying: 'Live
well to leave well.

What do you want to be remembered for? The fourth chapter of
the book asks this salient question. It is important we ask
ourselves this question. This book makes us realise that the

impact we make is what we'll be remembered for. How we affect people's lives is what we'll be remembered for. The writer has chosen her own path, which is charity. A value that was instilled in her by her parents' exemplary attitudes and the knowledge she acquired about the importance of giving. This, amongst numerous other good deeds are the things one should be remembered for. Living an impactful life is the most fulfilling aspect of our lives.

Aishah Adams opened our eyes to sadaqatul jariyah in the last chapter of this book subtitled: Get ready. Sadaqatul- jariyah is an everlasting sadaqah, which will outlive us after death. The prophet s.a.w mentioned that when the son of Adam dies, all his good deeds die except for three things which sadaqatul jariyah is part of.

Getting ready for death is like preparing for a long journey. You must take everything you need along with you. What are the things that'll benefit you after death? Aishah Adams connects our souls with the essentials that'll benefit us even after we're long gone. Sadaqatul jariyah, a continuous charity, like digging a well before you exit this world, it will outlive you. Other things that can outlive you are leaving pious children behind, benefiting others with knowledge amongst others.

Death is inevitable. We'll all die. Before death comes to us, the writer makes us know that we have responsibilities to discharge to dead muslims or dying muslims if we're opportune to be with them in their last moments. Part of our responsibility is to guide the dying person to say the kalimah, make their right sides face the qiblah, close the eyes of the deceased, cover the deceased amongst others.

The book, last call is an essential asset every Muslim must possessed. It prepares us for the inevitable journey. Death is the only reality that is certain. Nothing is certain in this life except death. How thoughtless can a human be? He prepares for uncertainties and leaves a certainty unprepared for. It is important we all start preparing for death. It's a reality that'll happen to us all. It's the last call for me and you.

May Allah bless Aisha Adams for putting this timeless book together. It will go a long way in assisting you and I to prepare for the inevitable journey.

Lateefah Adewunmi Jumah

Endorsements

Most People tend to run away or avoid the topic of death but I will tell you one thing, thinking and reflecting about death is one of the biggest way to create motivation and determination to live an intentional & amazing life in the pleasure of Allah. The Author offers us an invaluable gift of inviting us to remember the last call through her beautiful and insightful reflections laced with personal stories that brings the reader closer to understanding the message of the book. The book is reflectional, intriguing and just the right nutrition for our soul.

Hamdalah Sanni
Author, Coach, Speaker

The book,the last call is an essential asset every Muslim must possessed. It prepares us for the inevitable journey. Death is the only reality that is certain. Nothing is certain in this life except death. How thoughtless can a human be? He prepares for uncertainties and leaves a certainty unprepared for. It is important we all start preparing for death. It's a reality that will happen to us all. It's the last call for me and you. May Allah bless Aishah Adams for putting this timeless book together. It will go a long way in assisting you and I to prepare for the inevitable journey.

Lateefah Adewunmi Jumah
Author and Prolific Writer

As muslims, it is important for us to always remember the ephemerality of this world. The reality might not hit hard until we lose a dear one however, there are other subtle signs around us if we reflect enough. The author invites you to cultivate the habit of treating your life as a gift, and live it intentionally while preparing for the inevitable last call. Overall, it is a great job well delivered. We don't see so many books discussing death in such simple but engaging way.

Dr Khadijah Thanni
Medical Doctor and Author

In terms of the idea vis a vis correctness of message, the book is okay and I did not come across any errant ideas. Rather, it is a free flow message straight from the heart towards a preparation for the departure. It made a good read.

Imam Sulayman Fulani
Haafidhullah

This book **The Last Call** by my dear noble sister Aishah Adams (May Allah protect her) is simply an Admonition for those who reflect. Because I, personally was reminded in my course of reading it. The Author has put the books into five chapters:

Chapter 1 talks about Life being a gift and it should be treated at such. The way any individual will honour,acknowledge and appreciate gifts that is how everyone one of us should treat life by striving to make the best of it especially when is a temporary gift.

Chapter 2 talks about the inevitability of **death**. It reminds us of how transient life is. Especially when it happens to those who are dear and close to us. The Author gave us realities around that constantly reminds us of this **reality** no matter how subtle.

Chapter 3 talks about how prepared are we for death and what comes after it. It questions us regarding our plans and preparations for the inevitable journey. And the Chapter also mentions categories of people as relates to their preparation for the destroyer of pleasures.

Chapter 4 discusses about what do you want to be remembered for after your demise. This chapter helps to guide us on what to do and how to invest our time which will motivate us to have goals in life. And putting things in place along with dreams to achieve them. Interestingly ,the Author mentioned one of her goals, the Siddiqah Kitchens (May Allah bless it) which wa lillahi hamd, have been reaching out to thousands of the less privileged for over a decade now, we pray Allah elongate her life but is one major Legacy that she will be remembered for.

Chapter 5 : Get Ready! After going through this reminder and knowing about its reality, the next thing is to **Get Ready**!. The Author gave us tips that aid us in getting ready.

One thing I love so much about the book is, the author shared some many personal life experiences that is connected to The Last Call and it's preparation. Secondly, she gave us reflections at the end of every chapter which serves to cross check our dealings.

Lastly, May Allah reward our Author, Aishah Adams for putting up this work to remind us of this harsh reality which will be faced by every human who lives. That this world is limited and has an end and that end will come. The truth is that man hardly remembers death, unless a relative or a loved one passes away. This book is a must read for every one who believes in Allah and their return to Him. May Allah reward my dear sister Umm Aasiyah Aishah Adams with khayr in this world and in the hereafter.

Alhamdullillah wa Salatu wa salaam ala rasulillah .

AbuAmeenah Abd'Hakeem Inenemo

As someone who has experienced loss of many loved ones and also had a near death experience, I must say that this book is thought provoking and a much needed one right now. The truth is, we all think that we have time, but no we don't. At least, not as much as we think. The conscious awareness that death beacons, should motivate us to live our best lives. This book will show you how. Well done, The Mind Doctor.

Bashirat Abdulwahab
Author, Speaker, Coach

In the name of God

"Every soul shall taste death. And only on the Day of Resurrection shall you be paid your wages in full. And whoever is removed away from the Fire and admitted to Paradise, he indeed is successful. The life of this world is only the enjoyment of deception (a deceiving thing)."

Q3 ; VS 185

Dedication

This book is dedicated to The Ever Living, Al Hayyu Al-Qayyum; The One that will remain when all things perish. May His peace and blessings be upon the noblest of mankind, Muhammad ibn Abdullaah (sallallahu alayhi wassalam) who conveyed the message to us in its purest form.

I also dedicate this book to my parents who constantly remind me of good and bad deeds and made me conscious of death from an early age.

This book is also dedicated to three people dear to my heart who passed away around the same time;

Lamide Arogundade-Okin, Bro Niyi Sanuth (NS) and Alhaja Sote. We were hopeful however Allaah decreed and the Decree of Allaah is The Ultimate. May we be reunited in Jannatul firdaus Al-alaa. Aamiyn

Lastly, I dedicate this book to my dear grandparents who died upon the deen and who helped my parents before me stay upon the truth. May Allaah forgive them and all dead Muslims. Aamiyn. May He reunite us with our loved ones in Jannatu na'eem. Aamiyn.

Acknowledgement

I thank Allaah (subhaanahu wa ta'ala), my Lord and Master, The King and Master of the Day of Judgement, The Ever-living, The Most Merciful. I acknowledge that there is no deity worthy of worship except Him alone and I testify that Muhammad ibn Abdullaah (sallallahu alayhi wassalam) is indeed the final prophet and he (sallallahu alayhi wassalam) was sent with the truth.

I am extremely grateful to my entire family; first of all, my amazing parents. God consciousness was passed down to us through them. They were diligent in calling my siblings and I to His remembrance and worship. It was the little things, like making sure we learnt and said the dua'a for different events. We were not allowed to eat without saying a dua'a, or step out of the house without saying our dua'a; weekends were always for reflections and relearning until these habits became second nature to us. Only Allaah can grant them their reward in full for this love.

My siblings and I always enjoy deep and meaningful conversations and thus many of my thoughts and reflections on death would not have happened without them. For that I would always be grateful. May Allaah keep us united till Jannah. Aamiyn.

Many thanks to Dr H. O. Oseni for his love and words of wisdom which he shared freely. May Allaah honor him with Jannah. Aamiyn.

I am grateful to Abu Naasir (Hafidhahullaah) for the care and support he has shown over the years. I am also very thankful to Imam Suleiman Fulani (Hafidhahullaah) for taking time out of his busy schedule to review this piece and give advice; may Allah make your time spent in reviewing this book weigh heavily on your scales of good deeds. Aamiyn. I am also thankful to Br Samsideen Ige for all he has done to support my growth.

I am thankful to my beloved children, nephews and nieces for they are constant reminders that I am also moving close to my death and should thus impact on them positively. May Allaah make you attain greater heights than I ever did and make you leaders of those who remember Him much. Aamiyn.

I acknowledge my teachers from near and far whose gatherings of knowledge, advice and constant counsel have impacted on me positively. May Allaah honour you all in this world and in the hereafter. Aamiyn.

I acknowledge a few of my friends who have helped bring home the thoughts shared in this book. Whenever I was in that state of deep reflection and needed someone to unburden it to, they were never too shy or scared to speak about it with me- Kifaayah Umm Khadeejah, Lamide (Rahimahullaah), Segilola Sunmola and Olayinka Bakare. May Allah reunite us under His shade on that day when only His shade would suffice His creation and more importantly make our paths to Jannah easy. Aamiyn Big thanks to the many lovely people I have been privileged to meet on my journey so far who have in one way or the other added value to my life whilst helping me stay accountable, some of them have passed away and some are still here – Kofo Olokun-Olawoyin, Aisha Oloyede, Eniola Balogun, Aramide Fatoyinbo, Adeola Ajala, Jibril Okin and family, Ibrahim Sunmola, Rashidah Alli, Khadeejah Kokere, Muti'ah Badrudden, Aisha Mosuro, The Arogundades, The Olajobis, Dr Ahmad Abdullah, Hafsoh, Baderinwa, Zainab and Aisha Giwa, Jumoke Salami, Aisha Giwa (Rahimahullaah), Sr Summayyah Sadiq-Ojibara, Hameedah Kehinde, Mutiat Olaniyan, Ganiyat Bankole, Mariam Layeni and my lovely Siddiqah family. Many of these people I have constantly discussed or reflected on life and death with, while I have learnt from the death of others. May Allah forgive the dead amongst them and reunite us in Jannah.

Many thanks to Tope Ganiyah Fajingbesi-Balogun whose constant reflections on her father's death has caused me to think deep as well. May Allah forgive him and make his grave a place of rest. I also acknowledge the help and contributions of Hend Hegazi, Na'ima Roberts, Kaighla White, Ibrahim Mohammad, Aisha Mijindadi, Azeezah, Dr Rabiah Modile, Alhaja Fausat and Ndako. Your reward is with the Most High.

I am also deeply thankful to Omodara Adediran and her wonderful team, 'Aaishah (Umm Lubaabah) Abd-ur-Razaaq and Faizah Lawal-Tijani for being a pillar of support in getting this to the finish line. Special thanks to all my beta readers for the feedback and contributions. I really appreciate your time and words.

To every one of you, young and old who has helped me become a better version of myself; a more conscious Muslimah, your reward is with Allaah.

Verily, the stupor of death is real and it will come to us whether we prepare for it or not. May Allaah in His infinite mercies keep us in the life of this world so long as it is good for us and take us in death when it is best for us. Aamiyn.

Contents

Why Share Reflections On Death?

WHY am I writing about death?

Bismillaah.

Alhamdulilaah, wa salaatu wassalam 'alaa rasuullaah.

All praise is due to Allaah alone. May the peace and blessings of Allaah be upon the noblest of mankind, Muhammad ibn Abdullaah (sallallahu alayhi wassalam). Verily the best of words and guidance are from Allah (subhanahu wa ta'ala) and the best of examples is the Nabiy (sallallahu alayhi wassalam).

I testify that there is none worthy of worship except Allaah alone and I testify that the Nabiy (sallallahu alayhi wassalam) is His slave and Messenger. I am pleased with Allah as my Lord, with the Nabiy (sallallahu alayhi wassalam) as the prophet of Allaah and with Islam as my religion.

DISCLAIMER! I am NOT a scholar. I am NOT close to being referred to as a scholar. I hope to tow the part of these righteous people, past and present. May Allah grant me and every other person striving to achieve this lofty status ease. Aamiyn.

The next logical questions you as a reader would have

are; Why then have I chosen to write about such a deep topic? Why have I written this piece? What qualifies me to write on this topic?

What I share here are reflections and thoughts on the topic; DEATH! What I write here are some of the things I constantly speak to myself about and I share with you with the hope that you will read this and it will cause you to think deeply about life and live a more purposeful life. I write it with the hope that if I do not live to the age where I can really speak to my children about death as I'd love to, that they would find this book useful, reflect on it and live purposeful lives.

With the many deaths around us especially in recent times, as 2020 has been filled with many great tragedies around the globe, one would assume it would be an easy topic to have conversations on.

However it appears we haven't still woken up to a reality that would soon come true for us as well. I thus, write this with the hope that someone, somewhere would read this, ponder upon its content and be guided to live more consciously. If just one person is guided to live better by it, then In Shaa Allaah, my aim for writing would have been achieved.

Everyone who has learnt about death or any topic of importance owes it to themselves and the knowledge they have acquired to share what they know in the capacity and extent to which they know it.

The Nabiy (sallallahu alayhi wassalam) said;

"The search and acquisition of knowledge is an obligation laid on every Muslim."

However, it is also important to note that;

"In this social age, knowledge is only powerful when you share what you know"

-Charlie Helen-Robinson

It has therefore always been my resolve to share as much knowledge as I am able to as my way of leaving footprints in the form of good deeds whenever I leave this world.

I am a student constantly yearning to learn and share, constantly looking to benefit myself and others with the hope that perhaps someday, one of these would make me become elevated to the ranks of those beloved by Al-Wadud.

Death is a topic close to my lips and closer to my heart. My first encounter was sometime after high school. Of course, I had constantly heard of people dying; my childhood predisposition was that only old people died and of those old people, those who were good in this world would enjoy in the garden of Paradise while those who were bad in this world would rot in Hell-fire. However, my question was always this: what is the definition of good and bad? Who determines who was a good person and who was not? What is the yardstick that qualifies a person for paradise and another to the eternal damnation of hell-fire? Who sets this yardstick? Society? People? God? I mean we all watch the movies, where we root for the main actor who robs a bank, fornicates with the "Big Boss's" wife, and kills many people albeit bad guys, however we keep rooting for them because society says it is okay; they are the "Good Guys".

I definitely do not have the answers to the questions above. Although my parents constantly spoke to us about God and the importance of living a life of servitude, my young carefree self didn't take things seriously as I should have until after high school. The truth is that the signs are all around us. The answers are there for us, if we really want to know. Allah has said on the day of Judgement, there will be no excuse for the one who chooses not to acknowledge all we have been given and repeatedly shown. May Allah grant you and I beautiful lives and death. May He grant us the ease to see the truth, acknowledge it and take heed whilst we still can. because in the end…

Before I end this chapter, I would like to emphasise that any good found in this book is from Allah (subhanahu wa ta'ala) who makes good easy for whom He pleases and any shortcomings found herein is from none other than my nafs and I seek refuge in Allah from the whispering of the accursed. I seek the forgiveness of Allah for the errors found in this book.

I ask that He (subhanahu wa ta'ala) makes the benefits of this book weigh heavily on my scales of good deeds as well as scales of good deeds of all those who made this book a reality. May He (subhanahu wa ta'ala) forgive me, my family and loved ones (both known and unknown) and all dead Muslims. May He (subhanahu wa ta'ala) grant those of us still living steadfastness upon the truth till our last breath. Aamiyn.

And in the end, all praise is to Allaah alone, Al-Awwal wal Akhaar.

Aishah bint Abdulazeez Adams
August 16, 2020.
Lagos, Nigeria.

Prologue

All praises to the One who decreed death and life and made death a reminder for those who reflect. Many times, we feel we really understand the lessons embedded in the deaths around us; we say we have full grasp of what is to come, but do we really?

If life was to almost end right now, would you continue living the way you have been living? Would you continue to do all the activities you engaged in all this while? For some the reality has reached them. Below is an interview session with my sister and dearest friend, Lamide Arogundade-Okin, who passed away shortly after she granted me the interview. I had her permission to share this piece in my book and here it is. She passed on following a long illness and at the time she granted the interview she was full of positivity and hope and I was and still am very grateful to Allaah (subhaanahu wa ta'ala) for giving me the honour to have met such a wonderful person (Rahimahullaah).

I ask Allaah to make this interview beneficial and impactful and more importantly a hujjah for dear Lamide on the day it matters most. May Allaah grant her the highest level of Jannah and reunite us with her in Jannah, Aamiyn.

Interview with
Lamide Arogundade-Okin
(RahimahuLlaah)

Please note that the abbreviation AA is for me Aishah Adams, while LAO is for the late Lamide Arogundade Okin.

AA: As salamu alaykum

LAO: Wa alaykum salaam

AA: How are you doing today?

LAO: Alhamdulillah, always good.

AA: Thank you for agreeing to share with us. I am indeed humbled and grateful

LAO: It's always a pleasure.

AA: What dreams and goals did you have growing up? Have you been able to achieve them? How far or near are you from achieving them?

LAO: Growing up I guess some of our dreams were shaped by parents but situations change. One of my dreams was working with children and I believe that has been set in place already alhamdulillah.

AA: What is your state of mind like right now? How did it feel the first time you knew you had a terminal illness? How has the journey been since then?

LAO: Alhamdulillah I believe over the last few years I've

learned to stay positive and sincere in faith. When you deal with illnesses, it's important to remember that every soul shall taste death. Sometimes the fear of the unknown keeps us in a state not befitting of us especially as believers. We will cry, we will wonder where we went wrong but we must know and remember Allaah puts not on us a burden beyond which we cannot bear and there's a channel for that promised exit, so stay strong. Some other factors do affect how we react but the most important thing that carries us through is how we see Allah and relate with Him. Always be a thankful servant of the one who is capable in all situations.

AA: What is a typical day like for you right now? Is it any different from how it used to be before the diagnosis?

LAO: Of course, for us all life changes daily. But some circumstances make us realise somethings are more important than others. So, I'm more conscious about remembering Allaah, read more Quran; I'm more focused on achieving my goals. Make a bucket list if you like. I don't have one though, but keep yourself focused on doing what is reasonable for you.

AA: What advice do you have for us?

LAO: Don't let the feeling of "leaving a legacy" take your focus from what is most important. Allaah. Try to make sure your family remember something beautiful of you that leads them to remember Allah. Talk when you can, interact as positively as often too. Leave behind words they can remember you by.

AA: What are your hopes for the final moment or breath?

LAO: Just like everyone of us, we live between hope and fear. To be truthful beyond what most people seek of a good end with the kalimah on our last breath I believe our 'terminal' is in His hands so we do the best we can.

AA: What would you like your kids or loved ones to know that you've been unable to tell them?

LAO: Been unable? Well I just want them to always remember to worship Allaah alone and stick to the obedience of the Qur'an and Sunnah. Take guidance from the book of Allaah and I pray they continue commitment to Qur'an memorisation and acting upon it.

Food for Thought

I was extremely emotional when dear Lamide passed on. I remember I had a speaking engagement the very next day but I was still fazed by her death. I was emotional and distraught and was worried I wasn't going to be coherent on stage. A few minutes before going on stage, I spoke with a friend who had lost her mother during our semester exams in the university. I wanted to know how she was able to move on and focus on passing her studies despite the loss. She comforted me with her words and I remembered the final words Lamide said in her interview about wanting her loved ones to remember to worship Allaah alone and remain committed in their path. Those words resonated with me, and made me walk onto the stage to deliver a stellar speech. I hope this interview touched your heart as much as it did mine. On a final note my questions to you are;

*"What words do you hope to be
Remembered for and what are you
doing to leave your impactful
footprints behind?"*

"Death is not the biggest
disaster in life. The biggest disaster in life is
when our fear of Allaah dies when
we are still alive."
- Anonymous

1. Life Is A Gift, Treat It As Such

"He Who created Death and Life, that He may try which of you is best in deed: and He is the Exalted in Might, Oft-Forgiving"
(Q67 vs 2)

Ibn Abbas reported: The Messenger of Allah, peace and blessings be upon him, said,

"Take advantage of five before five: your youth before your old age, your health before your illness, your riches before your poverty, your free time before your work, and your life before your death."

{*Source: Shu'ab al-Imān 9575 Grade: Sahih (authentic) according to Al-Albani*}

Let me illustrate to you the power of gifts and how a singular act by my parents shaped my philosophy of receiving and giving gifts. When I was about 4 years old; while I was getting ready for the last day of school, my sister informed me that my dad asked to see me in his room. Naturally I thought I had done something, on getting to the room my dad responded to my greeting by giving me a shiny wrapped box. I was surprised and glanced at my mum for some sort of confirmation/clue. She was grinning from ear to ear. I remember jumping in excitement and rushed to hug my dad and thank him for my gift. He told me he had received my report card and was proud of my performance at school and wanted to surprise me. He sat me on his lap and said, "I wanted to see the joy in your eyes as you received this gift." He went on to tell me that my smile had made his morning even brighter.

I remember I made my siblings late for school that day because I had to unwrap the gift before leaving for school; in it I saw the most gorgeous pink doll which I wanted to sneak with me to show my friends but my mum caught me and made me return it to my room. There was also a pink notepad and pen; that was where I wrote my very first story and it was during that school holiday I discovered my passion for writing. I was super stoked for the rest of the day, actually scratch that, I was happy the entire school holiday and was determined to do even better the next school year.

A gift is something given to its recipient with the hope that they would find joy in it. A gift is something that should be acknowledged with delight, appreciated and kept sacred as best as the recipient can, at least that is the hope of the one who gives the gift.

Growing up, it was customary to give gifts and receive gifts. My parents encouraged us to make friendship bracelets for ourselves, draw cards and sometimes write poems for one another.

I was raised to always appreciate and acknowledge gifts no matter how small or tacky they looked (in retrospect some of those cards were made for the trashcan). Sometimes, we never got the gift we wanted, but we were taught to appreciate it regardless. Imagine how hurt my dad would have felt if after he had given me the gift, I had flung it under the bed somewhere or collected it rather grudgingly or even worse dropped it carelessly where it could be trampled upon by all and sundry.

There is a Yoruba adage that translate thus;

"A child that is grateful for today's
gift will get another tomorrow".

That has been my philosophy to the most beautiful gift of all;
The Gift of Life.

Life is indeed a temporary gift and we owe it to ourselves to honour it, acknowledge it and appreciate it whilst striving to make the best of it. To help you understand the extent of its importance, ask those who have lost their loved ones - if given a chance, how much would they be willing to part with to behold the face of their loved ones again or to hold them just one last time.

I never had the privilege of meeting my maternal grandmother as she passed away long before I was born. However, from the stories my mum has told about her, I know she was a phenomenal woman and I love her even though I never got to meet her. My mum is always full of tales about her life, and subconsciously I catch her teary-eyed staring into space almost as if she wishes she could see her again. I know if there was a halal way of seeing her just once (not the spooky hologram impersonation that most celebrities do nowadays), I would definitely explore. However, I know that isn't possible so I am patient and hopeful that we would meet joyfully in Jannah. In Shaa Allaah.

Why then aren't we who still have this precious gift of life appreciating it as we ought to? I'm not talking about having crazy bucket lists of skydiving or going on a 10,000 mile hike around the world. To appreciate your life as a gift would be to live it as best as you can whilst striving to earn the pleasure of your Lord, the Most High with every breath in you. To acknowledge it as a gift would be to treat time as sacred, we know that Time once lost can never be gotten back. To honour this gift would be to live an honourable life whilst striving to make our impact felt everywhere we are, however best we can.

Time passes by so quickly you know! One minute you are planning a huge event and then a few moments later it becomes past history. To put things in perspective, I look at my daughter and I remember when I was pregnant with her, I couldn't wait till 9 months was over and now my not-so-little-girl is going to high school. I mean where did all that time go? At some point, the biggest problems before you are what you'd like to be served for lunch and if your parents would allow you have as much of what you want as possible. At another time your problem is if you'd be able to provide the money for lunch for yourself and dependants. Subhaanallah!

Look at the children around you; notice how quickly their wants and needs change with time. In it is a sign for those who reflect. Look at your parents or the elderly around you; notice how they become softer and less demanding about certain things with time. Notice how they slowly age before your eyes yet time seems to stand still for the better part of the time except the last call – death strikes. In these are signs for those who reflect.

These days, I find myself reflecting on life. On constant replay are scenes from my past; scenes from my childhood, scenes from my high school days, events that occurred whilst I was in the University, people I met, things they/we did, things we shared, disagreements we had and how I could have done better. I reflect over mistakes that I made which altered things for me and those I did that were in my favour. And then I end up thinking about my afterlife- the life after death and what lies in wait for me.

Am I a *"Hollywood good guy?"* or am I truly good as my Creator has described mashallah. I wonder if all of my good deeds that I did with sincerity are accepted by Al-Adil, Al-Mujeeb or if I'd be found wanting; fa authubillaah that this happens to you and I. Aamiyn.

Life is a journey we all have been temporarily gifted with and it is important we acknowledge, appreciate and treat our life with care. We have to treat it as the gift that it is so we are not found wanting before Allaah, Al-Maalik on the day when only His sovereignty would reign. No one would have a tenable excuse on that day.

The passing of time is sufficient as a sign; the change and difference between night and day is a sign; the vastness of the land we live in is a sign; the climatic changes we constantly experience is a sign; the coming to life of the earth we live in after rainfall is a sign; the earthquakes and different kinds of natural disasters experienced across the world around us are signs; the life and death of the plants and trees is a sign.

Our challenge as human beings is not that we do not see and acknowledge the signs and wonders of Allaah (subhaanahu wa ta'ala), rather our problem is a lack of deep reflection on all that we see, hear and experience on our path to our final destination. We get carried away by the quick passage of time and do not stop to reflect over our actions and/or inactions. When the rain falls, we rush to take in our hung laundry instead of taking a moment to thank Allaah for the abundance of rain. When we are at the beach, we are quick to take out our phones to capture the beautiful scenery instead of taking that moment to appreciate Allaah for the clear skies. As human beings, we take for granted that we will live to see tomorrow or the day after, we assume that we would have enough time to make right our wrongs, make peace with those we have offended, have more time to spend with our loved ones when in reality no one is guaranteed their next breath. Allaahu Al-musta'an.

The problem is that we are in a hurry to experience life and our daily activities have become a never ending rat race;

Take a moment and just breathe...

Breathe in and exhale slowly...

Acknowledge that breath of air that just filled your lungs and thank Allaah (subhaanahu wa ta'ala) sincerely for it. Acknowledge its beauty and show gratitude to the One who gave it to you freely. If you have never had to struggle for breath to the extent of being aided by an oxygen tank, then you have one more reason to be grateful to Allaah, Ar-Rahman. If you are like me, who has been hospitalised and had your lungs fail you to the extent of needing to breathe with the aid of an oxygen tank, then alhamdullilaah we survived that ordeal, and are back to being able to take in deep fresh air unaided.

The truth is we get carried away by the ephemeral things of life to the extent that we fail to acknowledge what is right in front of our noses. This reminds me of some verses of the Qur'an.

Allaah says;

"The mutual rivalry (for pulling up of worldly things) diverts you until you visit the graves (I.e. till you die). Nay! You shall come to know! Again nay! You shall come to know! Nay! If you knew with a sure knowledge (The end result of piling up, you would not have preoccupied yourselves in worldly things). (Q 102 vs 1-5)

Subhaanallah! These verses are in a chapter many Muslims across the world have memorised. How many of us have stopped to reflect upon its meaning? How many of us have stopped to give it some thought? How many of us have striven to be guided by its message?

Although I memorized this verse in primary school and would recite it during prayers, I never knew its meaning nor bothered to check until one day while I was in university. It was Ramadhan of 2004; I was listening to the English translation of the Qur'an in my room when I heard the verse. Instinctively, I looked for the Arabic transliteration and realised that I had known this verse for as long as I had started learning to read the Qur'an in madrasah. I paused the tape and remained in a sombre state of reflection for some time after.

" ....wa khuliqal insana da'eefa"
And Man has been created weak
(Q 4 vs 28)

From the weakness of man is that he is forgetful and as you would expect life happened, time passed and I forgot this verse and its meaning until Allah made eeman (faith) settle in my heart. Verily man is forgetful except for the One Allaah guides to be conscious and upright. The beautiful things around us lure us, blur our vision and make us become heedless. Unfortunately, heedlessness benefits no one except the one determined to be from the people of the left hand on the day of judgement.

How then can we ensure that we stay focused on what should be our ultimate goal – Al-Jannah? How do we ensure that our time here on earth is spent in ways that show we cherish Allaah's Gift to us? How do we strive to live life purposefully for our Lord and ensure He is aware of our love and appreciation of all His Gifts to us? For He did not create all of this without intent and purpose for He (subhaanahu wa ta'ala) says;

"Do you think we created all of this
for play and amusement?"
(Q 23 vs 115)

Remember that life is priceless. Cherish every second you

spend here whilst you can. If you are reading this then it means you still hold His Gift of Life. It means you no longer have the excuse of not knowing what to do with it. It means you more than anyone else deserve to live better starting right now for tomorrow is not guaranteed for anyone.

When I was a child, I remember wondering why the elderly would make dua'a for long life. My late grandfather at over 70 years old would always make a recurrent dua'a for long life. He would say "O Allaah, grant us long life and good health," and I'd wonder why he was still asking for long life. Being the troublemaker that I was, I asked my grandfather if he wanted to live until he was 1000 years old like the tortoise in the bedtime stories he used to tell us.

Even the one who is granted respite till age 90 seeks to have respite for a longer time for every extra second is another opportunity to improve one's standing before Allaah on that day when nothing shall avail man or protect him from Allah's punishment except the one who meets Allah with a pure heart (qalbun saleem). Allah says;

" illa man atAllaha bi qalbin saleem"
(Q 26 vs 89)

I once entered upon my mum crying almost uncontrollably and in front of her were two books; her dua'a book and another bulky looking book. As I drew closer to her, I asked what was wrong. She just wouldn't stop crying. I remember she kept saying *"Had I known I would have come as a bird so I can be spared the test of that day,"* and she would cry some more. I heaved a deep sigh of relief; no one had died! I picked up the book she was reading and glanced at the opened pages. I realised her tears were brought on by what she'd read. She had been reading about the events of the hereafter and the day of reckoning and this caused her to cry profusely.

Anas ibn Malik reported: The Messenger of Allah, peace and blessings be upon him, led us in prayer one day. The Prophet turned to us and he said,

"O people, I am your leader. Do not precede me in bowing, prostration, standing, and turning. I see you in front of me and behind me."

Then the Prophet said,

"By him in whose hand is the soul of Muhammad, if you could see what I see then you would laugh less and weep more."

They said;

"O Messenger of Allah, what do you see?"

The Prophet said,

"I see Paradise and Hellfire."

{*Source: Ṣaḥīḥ Muslim 426 Grade: Sahih (authentic) according to Muslim*}

When was the last time you reflected over the events of the hereafter or do you think there is no life after this world? Do you think it all ends here? Do you think that the atrocities people seem to get away with whilst they are here would not be revisited? I am amazed by the one who cheats and spreads ill in the land almost as if their final home is this world; at the one that amasses wealth and treasures of this world like he will leave the earth with even a penny.

The afterlife is indeed more serious than we realise. If only we reflected upon the events that are sure to come, perhaps then we might start to reflect over our actions and/or inactions whilst we are here. Perhaps we would start to take our lives a bit more seriously.

Not everyone will have a wake-up call like Ali Banat (May Allah forgive him and have mercy upon his soul). Not many will have time to mop up their mess. Not many would be able to say proper goodbyes to their loved ones. Not many would be able to resolve mistakes they've made. Therefore, make every second count. Do as much good as you possibly can within the time frame you have.

Call that friend you need to call. Clear the air on issues you need to sort out if it's possible and if it's not, ask Allah to bring ease in rectifying the issues at hand whilst you can. Care for your family and loved ones with as much sincerity as you can muster. Leave people in a better situation than you met them and if you can't add value, please do not make it worse. Work hard at honouring your agreements. Strive to live a worthy life as best as you can.

Every single day, every minute, every second we spend, we are one step closer to our last breath. Every new breath you take is a promise that you will soon run out of life gas; it's a promise that the temporary gift of life would soon make its way back to the One who gifted you with it in the first place. Every new breath is a promise that the reality called death would soon strike. The beauty of the last breath would be determined by how well you lived your life.

May Allah call us back to Him when our meeting with Him is most beautiful with all our beautiful dreams fulfilled, our sins forgiven and our place in Jannah guaranteed. Aamiyn.

Reflections

◦*Life is a temporary gift that ought to be cherished-use it wisely.*

◦*We have been given this gift for a purpose- strive to fulfil it.*

◦*Death is certain for us all- never forget this reality.*

◦*Your life is a temporary gift, handle with care.*

Death is an impromptu exam
to be done on a date and time known to Allah
alone. Cherish life and live well while you can.
This life is touch and go so relate with it as
such;

Do not hold on too tightly to life like it's yours
for keeps

Remember the day your limbs would become
lifeless just as the soul has left its owner

Do not forget the day you'd sleep the final
sleep never to wake again

Verily this truth would come to us all
irrespective of if we are ready or not.

Remember that death is certain, the day of
accountability is certain, paradise is certain, the
questioning in the graves is certain, the stupor
of death is real, the fire of hell is real and our
living for eternity in the afterlife is true.

-Aishah Adams

2. Death Is Coming For You

"And the stupor of death
will come in truth:"This is what you
have been avoiding!"
(Q 50 vs 19)

The title of this chapter must sound pretty scary, right? I figured. However, it is the truth for every living thing. The moment you take your first breath at birth, death starts to make its way towards you; sometimes rather quickly, at other times slowly. Invariably, it meets up with you and hands you your "check-out" card. There is no time to rush back home to pack up a bag of deeds; there is no time to clean up whatever mess you've spilled on the floor; there is no time to pick up one last good deed or drop off any bad deed. Once death reaches you, you exit without the opportunity to improve on anything. You leave this world with nothing except your real inheritance of all you were given in this world- all of your deeds. Your only companion from this world would be what your hands have sent forth. How ready are you? Are you preparing for your catch-up with death?

Isn't it incredible how we spend so much time on every other thing except the on those issues that truly matter towards our afterlife? Isn't it surprising how we prepare for our weddings, naming ceremonies and other life events yet barely give the event of death much thought? Some people would rather talk to an inanimate object than have discussions about death and in the event they are forced to listen to discussions about it; they are in a hurry to leave such gatherings.

This brings to mind an incident that happened when I was in university. I was hanging out in a friend's room when a mutual acquaintance of ours stepped into the room. At the time she came in, I was engrossed in the book I was reading whilst paying no attention to the discussion going on in the room. Perhaps she had said something she expected me to respond to however I didn't catch it. This made her walk up to the bed I was lying on and she said to me;

"Please can I take a look at the title of your book, it must be really interesting since you appear to be taken with its content."

I internally chuckled and thought to myself,

"If only you knew."

At first, I didn't yield to her request as I was at a point in the book where I was in deep reflection and thus didn't want to drop the book. Eventually, I caved in and let her see the book. The moment her eyes caught the title on the cover of the book, she became hysterical and this amused me. I remember laughing at her facial expression whilst saying;

"What's with the scream?"

Her facial expression changed to one of deep disgust.

"Can you imagine what Aishah is reading with such rapt attention?" she asked the others in the room.

"She's reading a book on death; that's so morbid. You're really weird you know."

I remember responding along the lines of,

"What I choose to read or not read is my choice and you do not get to question it just because you choose to run away from the obvious."

It seemed ridiculous to me that she had gotten so upset about it. There are many who would react exactly the way she did. Not facing up to a reality doesn't make it untrue. We all will die eventually! This world is not our own, we are only here as passers-by and we are all on a trip towards our real home. Irrespective of whether we acknowledge the reality or not, death will come to us all.

We expect to live in this world like it's our permanent abode yet prepare nothing for our hereafter, hoping that God understands when we stand before Him. We hope that He (subhaanahu wa ta'ala) realises that we were really busy occupying ourselves with irrelevancies whilst we could have spent our time better acquiring wealth that would help us secure the most beautiful eternal home. Not knowing or truly grasping the seriousness of death and the finality that comes with it would avail no one when the last Call is made for your return.

Those who know me closely know that talking about death is something I tend to do quite so often. Initially, I was sceptical about discussing with others asides my siblings. This gradually changed after high school following some life changing events. Like most, I had heard about someone dying at different times whilst growing up however, I never understood the seriousness of it. Sometimes, when my parents needed to scold us for a wrong doing or tried to make us understand the implications of our actions, they would make us stage our own death. Don't be alarmed, it wasn't an extreme exercise. My mum would say something along the lines of,

"Close your eyes, what do you see? Darkness, right? Do you see me? Do you see your dad? – that is what would happen in the hereafter if you refuse to take heed and follow your desires."

The first time I knew how serious death was or losing someone could be was when I was in junior secondary. A family friend had lost her dad; I saw her sometime later at a mutual friend's house and it became apparent that things had become quite tough for them financially as a family after the death of her father because he was the sole breadwinner. I remember feeling bad for her and imagining what she was goinggoing through. I had seen many Nigerian movies of how the fatherless child would have to quit school to hawk oranges on the street to support their struggling mum. Thankfully, her case was very different but this made me appreciate my parents more. It made me more grateful they were still alive and healthy whilst silently praying that I wouldn't lose either of them. Alhamdulillaah, I have been spared the pain.

Subsequently, after I finished high school, it was December and there was the usual excitement and festivities that are accompanied with the end of a year. We woke that morning and I remember seeing my parents set out of the house early. It was after the pre-dawn prayers so I just went back to bed happily knowing I'd be able to sleep some more since there would be no need to prepare an early breakfast. I felt like I had slept for less than a minute when my sister angrily woke me up accusing me for sleeping despite what had happened. She told me that our cousin had died and our parents had rushed off that morning to pay their respects immediately after the pre-dawn prayers.

I was shocked at the news especially because he was barely in his 20s and seemed to have just started progressing in life. That was when I realised that death comes to people of all ages, race and ethnicity. Whilst my siblings and I were all sitting together reflecting on the tragedy, my older sister thought it best to share with us the events of the hereafter. I would call this my first proper introduction into the topic of the afterlife. You see, I have always looked up to my sister because she is knowledgeable in the Deen and always seeks for knowledge far and wide. That session was a much-needed wake-up call for us all. We couldn't go back to sleep that morning instead stayed up praying for our cousin.

As children, we were taught about the existence of paradise and hell-fire, however, I thought all would wait till the day of judgement. Before the knowledge sharing session with my sister, I didn't know that judgement began from the moment the last call was made. I didn't know there was life in the graves, SubhaanAllaah! Imagine my shock! My cluelessness at the time was not because the knowledge of it had not been shared with us by the Nabiy (sallallaahu alayhi wassalam), it was because I chose not to seek for it. The affairs of the hereafter are indeed true. The stupor of death is real and none would be saved from feeling it.

Some weeks passed and yet another 'call' was made. This time, someone I had seen quite regularly whilst I was growing up, our neighbour passed away. Inna lillaahi wa inna ileyhi rajiun. I remember hearing screams from the neighbour's house sometime in the middle of the night and they were calling out to my dad. I got up and went over to my sister's room and noticed she'd woken up as well. The screams and wailing kept us up and we kept wondering what had happened. This was a few hours before the pre-dawn prayers. The moment we offered the pre-dawn prayers, my parents made their way to our neighbours' where they discovered that he had passed on. This time I couldn't stop thinking about his sojourn to the afterlife. I couldn't stop thinking about his soul's current state and the fact that his judgement had begun. My hunger for more information about the afterlife, death and all that came with it had been born. Reflections on death and what came after helped me grow out of living a carefree life and I became more God-conscious. Losing my grandfathers, about one and a half years apart, pushed me further to pay attention.

Running away from reading and learning about death is like avoiding to study for your school exams. Irrespective of whether you're prepared or not, you'd be served the exam papers once it's time to begin the exam. I strongly believe that because Allaah (subhaanahu wa ta'ala) loves us all, He helps us remember death often and gives us constant reminders, however subtle. It is therefore our obligation to be aware of them. Death is sufficient as admonition for the one who truly cares about his eternal home.

Have you ever seen a corpse, whether in real life or in a movie or perhaps the internet? Did you notice how their beauty and status became irrelevant? Have you ever looked upon the face of a person dying slowly from an illness, or perhaps acute hunger like in the UNICEF relief campaigns, notice how their cheek bones cave-in and the glow they once had fades away?

I remember seeing pictures of a famous actor after his body was recovered from a ghastly car crash. He was absolutely unrecognisable; as if to help us remember him, the journalist put a picture of him alive next to a picture of his corpse.

Look at us, strutting across the earth in arrogance, acting as if we own our life while the Owner of all that exists watches us patiently, hoping we would take heed and live purposefully. Look how we joyfully acquire 'toys' that may lead to our death and destruction yet we don't acquire as much of those things we'd continue to benefit from long after we are dead and buried.

Death is inevitable for us all. The knowledge of this shouldn't make us live in constant fear because the real fear is standing before our Rabb and being found wanting despite all the opportunities we had to live better. Our efforts should be in striving to live more meaningful and impactful lives. No one knows when the hour of the day of judgement would come. How prepared are you for the last call? How prepared are you or your appointment with death?

One day you are sitting lovingly in the company of a friend or loved one and the moment this person passes on you suddenly become scared of being in the same room with them. This is that person who you'd probably have spent a long time with without wanting to leave their side. Isn't that enough as admonition for us to be more fearful of our standing and less concerned about what people think or say. The same person who seems to love you so much – not wanting you to do certain religious practices when you are alive would abandon you the moment death strikes. In the end, you'd face your Lord all by yourself with no helper. What then is your motivation for your actions?

Are you motivated by the actions of some friends who appear to be cool and living the life or are you motivated by family honour thus dishonouring others in the process? Are you motivated by sincere love for good deeds or are you carried away by the temporary acquisition of worldly benefits? Allaah (subhaanahu wa ta'ala) says;

> *"Beautified for men is the love of things they covet;*
> *women, children, much of gold and silver (wealth),*
> *branded beautiful horses, cattle and well tolled land. This is*
> *the pleasure of the present world's life; but Allah has the*
> *excellent return (paradise with flowing rivers) with Him*
> *(Q 3 vs 14)*

He (subhaanahu wa ta'ala) also says;

> *"...and give glad tidings to the patient"*
> *(Q 2 vs 155)*

All of the things we see and accumulate around us will fade away and become only a memory. All you'd have left would be your deeds.

I paid a dear friend a visit sometime back and I saw the car she used to drive when we were in school sitting in the driveway. It had been at least 10 years since the last time I saw her drive the car; as you would imagine, it was relegated to the corner of the compound, tyres deflated, dust accumulated. There was a tray of egusi (melon seeds) on its rooftop, left there to dry. While walking out to my taxi, we passed by the car and subconsciously both said Inna lillaahi wa inna ileyhi rajiun at the same time. We looked at each other and started laughing. It was apparent in that moment we were thinking the same thing. We talked about how "cool" the car had made her seem in university and the multiple free rides she gave me. I asked why she didn't sell it or give it out, and she laughed and told me no one would be happy to receive it, as it would be more of a financial burden than relief on them.

Think back at the things that used to matter to you at some point; the hang out joints you would break a limb to go to; the things you'd be most elated to acquire – how do you feel about them now? Seasons change all the time. Everything would pass away with time. Everything would lose its value except that which Allah chooses to preserve. Everything would perish except the Face of Our Lord Most High.

Death is coming for you so spend your time doing as much good as you can whilst you still have time here with as much sincerity as you can muster. You can never go wrong serving Allaah (subhaanahu wa ta'ala) according to His teachings and laid down rules.

You will be tested; you will experience pain and anguish however all these are part of the trials and tribulations of the life of this world so stay strong and hold firmly to His rope, however hard it might be, till the last call is made. Verily Allaah is the best of those who reward.

Attach yourself to His remembrance and worship Him

having firm faith in His promises for He is AlHaqq. This world is not our own, we are only here for a given time. Make every second of your time here count knowing that Allah would not allow the deeds of anyone of us go unrewarded. He is indeed The Truthful, The Generous.

How many have wished their time here was extended when death drew close. While some are warned of the nearness of death, many aren't. Many people leave home and are met with a ghastly road accident, many people slump in their bathrooms while taking what should be a harmless shower. We shouldn't assume that death will come due to a pre-existing illness where we would have time to sort our affairs, or that death will come when we are old and frail on our bed in our sleep. Irrespective of what category we eventually fall into, let us work towards making our exit from this world memorable to those we leave behind. My dad always used to say to us "Make your presence felt anywhere you go or leave." Let your absence be noticed by virtue of the fact that you impacted on the lives of people positively.

Building skyscrapers with your name boldly written on them does not engrain your name in the hearts of people; being hardworking and famous does not keep you in the heart and minds of people. However, living and relating with people with sincerity and kindness keeps you in the heart of many. Sincerity has a way of making a person's good deeds more valuable in the sight of many as Allaah *TabarakAllah* loves deeds that are done with sincerity of intentions. Wishing others well and striving to be of help, seeking no thanks from them however seeking the Face of your Lord increases the value and depth of your deeds. Sincerity in relating with people does NOT mean that you will not have fall outs nor does it mean you will not get angry at yourselves- in fact you will. However, sincerity means that even when you disagree, Allaah (subhaanahu wa ta'ala) aids you to be remembered in a good way when you're away from them.

I grew up in a home where the brand of love freely shared was **tough** love. When at the receiving end of this brand of love during a trying time, it can be really frustrating however if there was ever a set of people I can never get out of my mind or prayers- it's my family.

No one likes to have their shortcomings under the spotlight; feedback could be a hard pill to swallow however paying attention to them, improving on them whilst striving to make the world a better place helps you stay in the minds and memory of people for much longer.

Reflections

Ibn 'Umar also said that Allaah's Messenger, (sallallaahu alayhi wassalam), said;

"You should remember the reality that brings an end to all worldly joys and pleasures, namely, death."

(Hadith is narrated by At-Tabarani with a sound chain of narrators)

○*Death is on its way towards you, get ready!*

○*Acquire deeds that make your absence noticed.*

○*The stupor of death is more real than the book in your hands.*

○*In the end, all you really have to yourself are your deeds, invest in them.*

Live in this world as a stranger
while striving to be amongst the
honoured ones in our permanent
home; the hereafter.
"He who fails to plan, plans to fail"
— Anonymous

3. What Preparations Are You Making?

*"Proper preparation is the
prerequisite for any
successful activity"*
Anonymous

Ibn ' Umar reports: "I came to the Prophet, peace
be upon him, and I was the tenth of the first ten
people (who embraced Islam). A man from
among the Ansar got up and said:

"O Prophet of Allah, who is the most sagacious
and the most prudent among the people?"

He replied:

*"Those who are most aware of death and prepare
themselves for it. They are the wisest of people and
will have honour in this world and a generous
reward in the Hereafter.""*

(Hadith is narrated by At-Tabarani with a sound chain of narrators)

One of the first important trips I ever made was when I was
going to resume boarding school. Before then I had gone on
short trips always in the company of family the entire trip. This

particular trip was one in which I was 'going into the world' to make my mark, or so I was made to believe.

I prepared for boarding school for weeks. From the moment my results were released, we started making preparations since it had become apparent that I was one of the successful candidates. There was a long list of items every student was expected to bring. My parents bought all I needed and also assisted me in getting ready. We packed, checked to be sure all was intact and cross checked close to the day of departure for school. My school was in a different state from where I lived, this meant it was a long drive to get there and I would not be allowed to go home on weekends or whenever I felt homesick. I had a myriad of emotions; I was excited and scared all at the same time but was optimistic and expectant of the journey ahead.

How much preparations are we putting in place for the inevitable journey? How much planning and cross checking are we doing to ensure that once the time comes for us to go, we are able to move without any excuse as to why we should be given extra time or time to quickly pick up valuables we forgot to take along.

Our 'valuables' for this journey towards death are our deeds; all of them. How much preparation is being put in place to ensure we aren't found wanting during our 'interview' session with the angels that would question us in our graves?

I have a friend who literally has a spread sheet for every intended new venture or activity. This friend of mine once told me how detailed the spread sheets usually were. Do you have a spread sheet detailing how you hope to spend your time here? Do you have back up plans for those aspects of life that matter? I do not have spread sheets like my friend; I would not claim to be that organised. However, I have set goals and timelines for the things I'd like to do and by when I hope to achieve those goals. This helps me to evaluate myself, it helps me gauge how well I am doing; it helps me track my progress. It also helps me call myself to order whenever it's obvious that I am lagging behind. What preparations are you making towards your final exit? It does not matter whether you use spread sheets or milestones, what matters is that you have a method of calling yourself to check whilst keeping in mind the knowledge that your exit draws near.

What expectations do you have for your life in the grave? What expectations do you have for your life in the hereafter? Are you giving the matter any thought or do you hope to just go with the flow when the time comes? The wise one is he who keeps in mind the coming of the hour and prepares for it. The smart one plans their life towards their time of death. Being too scared to think about it would not stop you from experiencing it. Being uninformed about the events that follow would not prevent you from being called – ready or not.

It is amazing how we seem to research everything except death. When you are going to a new school, you probably study the school's brochure to get a feel of what to expect. When you were going to get a job, you probably researched the company to understand their modus operandi; you probably even met with people working there prior to you joining to be well informed and guided on how to proceed.

Preparations for our last call should be more detailed than for this is THE most important call. You will be resurrected the way you passed away you know. How do you want to exit? When do you want to exit? In what way would you love to exit? Ever thought about this? What preparations are you making to ensure you exit in the manner of your dreams?

Imagine you are on a train full of passengers. The train sets out and then at every stop along the way, people alight; young, old, weak, strong, middle aged- basically people of all class, age, colour and race alight. Ever stopped to observe the different people and the different ways in which they get off a train? I have. In my reflections on death, I have sometimes gotten lost in thought at train stations and I have observed the different ways people get off (I probably shouldn't have been so engrossed one day because I missed my stop).

Some are ready and standing at the door prepared to get out of the train the moment it gets to their stop. They look around the train to be sure they didn't leave behind anything of value. They get set early and step off the moment the doors open. These set of people are usually composed and calm once they are off the train. I'll call them the **"Smart Planners"**.

Another set of people start to get ready, the moment they notice the train is approaching their stop However, for a few minutes before the train gets to their stop they get carried away and then call themselves to check just before the train gets to their stop. Of course, they have to get up and be by the door of the train amidst a rush and get off quite flustered and all over the place. I'll call these ones the **"Unstable Dislodgers"**.

There are those who get carried away with the beautiful distractions in the train however they are able to call themselves to order in time to disembark; amidst a rush they get to the door of the train just as it's about to open. They manage to calm themselves and stay composed as they get off. I call these the **"Fortunate Dislodgers"**.

There are also those passengers who could not be bothered whether the train is approaching a stop or not, they sit and make merry in the train almost like they would not be alighting from it. From the moment they get on the train to the moment they get off; they are carried away with the trappings present there on. Although in reality no one drags you off a train except you didn't pay your fares or you were being a nuisance, these set of passengers despite not defaulting in the way that is obvious get dragged off the train amidst their plea for more time to quickly pack up their stuff and clean up their mess. I call these ones the **"Unfortunate Dislodgers"**.

And there is the last group I refer to as **"Spectators"**. They get on the train and get carried away with the happenings therein. They focus less on the direction of the train and seem to be watching this person and that person. They are more focused on what is going on with other passengers on the train, this makes them lose track of time thus having a similar fate to the unfortunate dislodgers.

Which category would you like to be in when you disembark from the train of life? What are you doing to ensure you are a smart planner and not a spectator? Wouldn't you like to be prepared and ready when death enters upon you? Wouldn't you like to be calm and composed when the angels wake you up in your grave to answer the interview questions? How beautiful would it be if you and I are from the fortunate ones when we leave this world? What have we prepared for that hour? What preparations are you engaged in to guarantee your readiness?

Not being ready would be unacceptable. For some death comes suddenly, for others it comes with a short warning sign; yet for some others they are given time to get set and say their goodbyes before they depart. We do not know what the morrow holds for us but we can plan towards it.

I hope that I would have some time to say my farewells; I hope I would exit this world whilst in the company of my loved ones. More importantly, I hope that I would exit when the last of my deeds would be my best deeds ever. Have you given some thoughts to how you'd like to exit? Are you working towards having it happen that way by staying true to Allaah and worshipping Him with sincerity?

Every time I hear of the passing of someone; irrespective of whether I knew them closely or not, I ask for the cause of death. At some privileged times I get a full narrative of how they departed. These narratives are channels that lead to deep thinking and reflections. I start to wonder how the departed soul felt as they made their final exit; I wonder if they were calm or scared; I wonder at their joy or sorrow at the meeting with their Lord and more often than not I worry about how they are faring in their graves. I wonder if I'd have gotten my desired beautiful exit if I had left when they did. For some time afterwards, I'm often in a state of worry and panic wondering what admonition their death has tried to tell me, wondering if I had truly grasped the message the news of their death came with. I believe events that happen around us are there for us as signs and if we truly reflect, we would be the better for it.

I recall the first time I saw a corpse. It was that of my grandfather, the one I thought would live till he was 1000years old. I received a call whilst in university of the passing on of my paternal grandfather and immediately set out to meet up with the rest of my family. He passed away on a Friday morning and my father saw no reason to delay the Janaazah beyond the 'asr prayers of that day. My dad is well known for his time consciousness so everyone rallied round to make it happen. When we arrived at my grandfather's residence his body was being washed. Shortly after his shrouded body was brought out and placed on an elevated space in the sitting room. I kept looking at his body thinking, this is really it? This is truly the end for him? After the Janaazah prayers, I watched how everyone left his graveside and went about their duties almost as if nothing tragic had happened. Yoruba (an ethnic group in the south west of Nigeria) have an adage that says;

'eni to kuu nii tiye gbe'

Meaning;

**"the departed soul is the one who
has experienced doom"**

Subhaanallah. everyone turned away and left him to His accountability. His house stood right there, his room was now

38

Empty with only his clothes and personal effects as signs of what used to be his presence.

Imagine the swiftness with which the body is discarded (cast) into the graves once the soul departs; notice how people are in a hurry to leave the graveside. Isn't that sufficient for us as admonition? I concluded that day that *no one* is worth disobeying Allaah for *-no one!* I recalled a lecture where the scholar said;

"You will die the way you lived;
you cannot fool Allaah."

Laa hawla walaa quwatta illa billaah. Again, I ask, how would you like to die? Have you started giving it some thought? Would you like to die peacefully in your sleep or would you like to pass on after a brief illness? Would you like to die a martyr or would you like to pass on whilst in sajdah to Allaah (subhaanahu wa ta'ala)? Would you like to pass on while reclining in the masjid reciting from the words of Allah azza wa haal or would you like to pass away whilst having a nice time hanging out with family and friends. Invest your time doing that act you'd like to be called back from. I believe that part of our preparations for the last call should involve giving some thought to how we'd depart so we can ask Allah to bless us with our desired beautiful end in the way we seek. And as we seek this from Him, we stay true to His worship and remembrance.

Some time ago, I read the story of a sister who passed away and it was observed that her clothes appeared longer than usual. During the shrouding of her body, the same was the case. Although the shrouding used for her was for her exact body size, it kept extending beyond and so she was eventually buried like that. Those who witnessed these mysteries were perplexed so they mentioned their observations to the family and upon enquiry it was reported that she always supplicated to Allaah to grant her shroud an extra length in such a way that would not leave her uncovered. SubhaanAllah. She asked from Allah, stayed true to Him and Allaah was true to her. Allaah accepted her dua'a for verily He is Semiu dua'a.

Striving to leave people in a good state is also one of the preparations we need to make towards our exit. Every matter we leave unresolved would have to be resolved on the day of judgement. Yes, some people are rather difficult to deal with and so it might be foolhardy to even attempt to settle scores with them. However, make efforts to depart from people leaving them in a good state.

I met up with a friend once when I got back from Umrah some years ago and she told me about the passing of a mutual friend and her narration of the event impressed upon me the importance of refraining from keeping malice and leaving issues unresolved. She and the late sister were close friends until they had an altercation. This had made them cut off relations with themselves for a while. Less than two weeks before the sister's demise unbeknownst to them, my friend summed up courage and reached out to the sister. Alhamdulilaah they were able to resolve issues and the air was cleared between them. Subhaanallah, upon the sister's demise my friend was one of those who washed her body in preparation for the grave! She said to me "I was shaking the whole time and I kept thinking what if I hadn't resolved issues?" As she narrated the incident to me, I could see she was still deeply moved by the occurrence. She kept saying "Imagine if we still had our issues." That was a pivotal moment for me. Now just stop and think about this for a second, what if they still had unresolved issues when the sister passed away? *Alhamdulilaah* she was fortunate to sort things out; not many are that lucky. There have been instances where the two people in disagreement with one another meet their death at the same place whilst being at war with each other. The currency that day would be our deeds. *"I am sorry"* would not avail anyone once they cross over to the hereafter. Strive to part with people as peacefully as you possibly can, there might be no second chances or extra time to sort things out once we get to our stop.

Putting our finances in order is another worthy preparation to make so as not to be caught pants down - especially our debts. It amazes me when I hear someone say, *"I forgot all about the debt"* -how can you forget? Whenever I am in debt, I am unable to sleep well at night. I am perpetually in a state of worry and fear whilst begging Allah to grant me ease to repay. I am usually so worried death would catch up with me before I pay up. When the worry gets to a head, I usually would call the person I'm indebted to, to find out if the debt would be forgiven upon my demise. I would hate to part with any of my good deeds. How then can you forget you owe or treat the one you're indebted to with impunity?

I had a discussion with my sister about this and she laughed at my concern. Being forgetful of your debt is like being forgetful of your meeting with your Lord. What seems worse than being nonchalant of your indebtedness is short-changing others in your dealings with them. A whole clan (the people of Saalih) was wiped out by Allaah because of this, yet people handle this matter with levity.

Being deceitful in dealings has become wide spread yet vastness in wealth has not increased. Isn't that a reason to reflect? Let's even say you claim to short-change others in your dealings with them in the name of struggling to make ends meet for yourself and family (not that there is any justification for this), what is your excuse when you exploit your own family?! There is NO valid reason to short-change others neither is there a reason to be unbothered about honouring your trusts.

Yes, Allaah has granted some more ease than other so this is not about not owing at all; it's more about striving to pay as soon as you can. In the event things don't turn out as planned; acknowledge your debt, be apologetic about your delay in repayment and strive to return the loan as soon as Allah grants you ease. Our standing before Allah is more serious than we realise and so adequate preparations need to be made to ensure we are not found wanting when our time comes.

Reflections

◦ *Would you like to be a smart planner, an unfortunate dislodger or a spectator?*

◦ *How would you like to disembark from the train of life? A smart planner, an unfortunate dislodger or a spectator?*

◦ *Work towards having the end of your dreams by living the way you'd like to end.*

"The future belongs to those who believe in the beauty of their dreams"
-Eleanor Roosevelt

4. What Do You Want To Be Remembered For?

"When a man dies, his deeds are cut away except three, continuous charity, beneficial knowledge and righteous children that remember him"
(Sahih Bukhari and Muslim)

It was a bright Friday morning; the students of the adult madrasah were gathered at the venue of the weekly study circle. Our teachers were also waiting for us to settle down so the session could start. When it was time, to start off, Abu Hudayfah shared with us the hadith we were to learn and discuss for that day. The hadith quoted above was the hadith we memorised that day. Alhamdulilaah, it has stayed with me since then.

I was raised by my parents to be an achiever. We were raised to aim high, strive as best as we can and die whilst working towards achieving our set goals. My intent to exemplify the above quoted hadith further reinforced this upbringing.

When I was 4 years old, I had a discussion with my mum and it set the pace for how I started to relate to life events later on. My siblings and I used to act out our intended future professions and I would act out the part of a nurse. My elder brother, the skilled artist, had drawn a caricature that looked like me in my nursing gab and so I excitedly went off to show my mum. Upon seeing the drawing, she asked, why I wanted to be a nurse and not a doctor. I naively blurted out "Because women cannot be doctors." You see, based on all the cartoons I had seen, I assumed 2 things: that women could not be doctors and men could not be nurses. She was surprised I had formed that opinion and so she educated me about stereotypes and more importantly told me that women could be doctors and in fact I could be anything I set my mind to being provided I worked hard at it. I smiled and told her I had changed my mind and was going to become a doctor Inshallah. While I am in no way saying that being a doctor is the ultimate and superior to being a nurse or any other profession, however, this is merely to illustrate how I could have developed a second-best mindset and learned to settle for less if my mum hadn't assisted me in overcoming stereotypes. I realised that I had what it takes to be whoever I wanted to be irrespective of the cultural conditioning around me.

Notice how she gently but firmly planted the seeds of confidence and helped me embrace being the best version of myself. This has stayed with me ever since and each time I want to achieve a goal, I find out what the best is and I work towards it. That doesn't mean I never encountered difficulties. Whenever I was feeling overwhelmed and anxious about an impending project my dad would say; "Aishah you have a million reasons to fail but not a single excuse." I have since learnt that one of the biggest setbacks of many for being unable to achieve their set goals is making excuses.

Learning the hadith has guided me on what to do and how to invest my time. It has been my guide and I fine-tuned my life goals and dreams around it with the hope that I'd be able to leave behind the 3 things mentioned. I would implore you to do the same while teaching your loved ones as well. Before learning the hadith, one of my ardent wishes for my life had always been to strive to leave my footprints in the sands of time. However cliché that may seem, I had always been focused on leaving a good legacy and thus my actions and deeds have always been towards achieving a lot in this dunya such that I will be remembered fondly by people and quite frankly I seemed to be all over the place in my bid to achieve this mark. However, after listening to the sermon and learning the hadith, the "how" in terms of what actions and deeds I needed to do in making my impact became clearer after that study session. This is part of the epiphanies that birthed the *Siddiqah Street kitchen*.

What would you like to be remembered for?

This is a question you need to give a lot of thought to as I did. If you never thought about this before now you might become confused on which way to direct what your answer should be. Be guided that whatever you do, ensure that your choice(s) are beneficial to you even in the grave long after you're bones and decayed in the earth. Whatever you decide to do with your life moving forward, ensure it is in line with the things that are permissible because you will be as you'd be called to account for that which people copied from you of evil and wrongdoing. May Allaah forgive us for all we've done to 'inspire' others to disobey Him. Aamiyn.

What actions of yours would you love to be ingrained in the memory of others? What nickname(s) would you like to be known by which explains what you're living your life for? There are so many things I'd like to achieve and be remembered for. In order for us to achieve our dreams, we must first believe in our abilities to see them through.

Deciding early the course I wanted to tow (i.e. leaving my footprints in the sands of time) meant that I had to study the lives of some of the amazing people whose names have not been erased from history even though they passed on over a decade ago. I had to choose exemplary figures whose lives are worthy of emulation not because of their beauty or brains; not because of their wealth or family name; not because of their lineage or cliques but because of what they did with what they were blessed with of beauty, brains, wealth and status. They are remembered because they strove to make the world a better place using their wealth, fame and status to serve others. They used the resources at their disposal to ensure that their impact was felt.

My question to you is;

What are you doing with your gifts and resources?
Is it making you become conceited and oppressive
or are you ensuring others are living better lives
by virtue of your help?

The beauty of a person's life is not in its longevity but in the richness of its quality which is observed from how well they lived. Have you ever pondered on why a kind-hearted person would be likened to *Mother Theresa*? A gentle person would be likened to *Mahatma Gandhi*? How many times have you seen people remember famous singers or fashion designers that passed away? This is not to say fashion designers aren't doing the fantastic work of making lovely clothes that cover us up, however, how many of these slay queens or cloth gods held your hearts beyond the initial period of their demise? You can be in the hearts and minds of people with whatever amazing skill you have so long as the intention behind it is to seek His Face and the actions are in line with His teachings.

In deciding to leave my footprints in the sands of time, I studied the lives of the sahabahs (radiyAllahu anhum) and I chose my role model to be our mother, Aaishah (radiyAllahu anha). Alhamdullilaah my parents named me after this phenomenal woman. I started working towards mirroring her life, though I am very far from where I'd love to be, I am along the path, striving and hoping that someday, one day, I'd get to my destination, hopefully before I leave this earth.

Some of the things I hope to be remembered for were nurtured from an early age. May Allah forgive my parents and grant them increase in good for all the good examples they set for us. My dad is married to only my mum; this has always been the case yet my house was almost like the set of *'Fuji house of commotion'* -a Nigerian soap opera I used to watch as a child. We were about 30 people living in the house at some point and my parents were responsible for at least basic upkeep and maintenance of all these people. My parents would open their doors to the helpless and needy provided they were harmless and would not steal or endanger our lives. A good number of these people had no blood ties with us yet they were assisted to improve their lives. This opened my heart to showing love to people irrespective of religion or blood ties. What further cemented the love for sharing and caring were 2 hadith I learned later in life;

Jabir reported: The Messenger of Allaah, (sallallaahu alayhi wassalam), said;

"The food of one person is enough for two, the food of two is enough for four, and the food of four is enough for eight."

{*Source: Ṣaḥīḥ Muslim 2059 Grade: Sahih (authentic) according to Muslim*}

Also, Al-Nu'man ibn Bashir reported: The Messenger of Allah, (sallallaahu alayhi wassalam), said;

"The parable of the believers in their affection, mercy, and compassion for each other is that of a body. When any limb aches, the whole body reacts with sleeplessness and fever."

{*Source: Ṣaḥīḥ al-Bukhārī 5665, Ṣaḥīḥ Muslim 2586; Grade: Muttafaqun Alayhi (authenticity agreed upon) according to Al-Bukhari and Muslim*}

These are the hadith of the Nabiy (sallallaahu alayhi wassalam) yet how many are acting in line with them? It is my belief that if we were truly exemplifying this then the rise in depression and suicide in our communities would be non-existent. How are you with your family? How are you with your neighbours? How are you able to turn your face away from one obviously in need of food and shelter when you have the means to help? How do you sleep well at night knowing the food you considered as waste and just trashed would have put smiles on the faces of others?

One of the things I'd like to be known for is found in the words of Allaah in the Qur'an.

Allaah says;

"And they give food, inspite of their love for it
(or for the Love of Him), to the poor, the orphan,
and the captive. (Saying): "We feed you seeking Allah's
Countenance only. We wish for no reward, nor thanks
from you. Verily, we fear from Our Lord a Day, hard and
distressful that will make the faces look horrible
(From extreme dislike to it)".
(Q 76 vs 8- 10)

Food is a basic necessity. Hunger and starvation are the main cause of death for millions of people across the world. I watched a documentary on how impoverished Haitians eat cookies made from dirty mud; these cookies have no nutritional value but at least manage to keep the poor people alive. As an empath who was fortunate to be raised in a home of givers, giving and sharing with others had always been second nature but as imperfect humans there was still that bit of resentment and unwillingness to part with an item, or toy or cloth even though I didn't really need it. Reflecting over the verses of the Qur'an I learnt helped me start to let go. Now as an adult, as a rule, every 6 months I declutter my house. In my pantry there are food items I have bought for the sake of trying a new recipe that I never got around to trying, in my wardrobe there are dresses I always believe I will wear even though I wear the same set of jilbabs almost every day, in my children's toys stash there are new toys they just couldn't be bothered playing with. All these and more are some of the items I love to give out without doing a garage sale.

I came across a narrative about Aaishah (RadiyAllahu anha) once and I was deeply moved by her kindness and generosity. She had been fasting however she was one who lived to give so she gave of her provisions freely to the point she had given out all the food in her house at the time. Her slave girl had to remind her of the fact that she was fasting and she had left nothing for herself to break the fast with! She (RadiyAllahu anha) had faith in the provision from Allah and she remained calm.

Many times, when I withhold from giving a certain thing, I often later realise I could have survived without it as that thing I held on to usually goes to waste or remains dormant from unuse. One of my respected guardians used to say to me,

> "Whatever we spend freely of what we
> have or use for ourselves and others is what
> is truly ours and that which we hoard or
> choose not to use is for our inheritors."

SubhaanAllah. There is NO guarantee we'd eventually get to spend or use that which we hoard so why hoard when we can bring ease to others through it.

This is NOT to say that we should not save for tomorrow. This is also not to say we should not be wise in how we spend. What I mean to say is – make the best use of your resources whilst ensuring your presence is felt by helping others as best as you possibly can.

Reminds me of an incident that happened some years ago.

My friend and I had gone in search of funds for a project we were working on; we had an appointment at the residence of one of our intended benefactors. We got to the house just as the family were at the breakfast table and we were invited to join. As we sat at the table, I noticed the serving bowls had at least 3 different meals and we were told they were about to conclude breakfast. Upon hearing that, I exchanged looks with my friend and kept mute. The table had 'leftover' food that was enough to feed at least 5 more people. The cook was asked to bring back some of the dishes he had taken off the table and we were offered food alongside 2 others who joined while we were there. We all ate to our fill and there was still some left. On our way back to our house, I was deep in thought. I kept pondering on what would have happened to the food we ate if we had not turned up. Would it have ended up in the bin?

Many times, we hold back from giving when what we have is more than enough for us and our family. If you have ever tasted hunger, homelessness or hopelessness, I wonder how you sleep well when things get better for you without looking around to help others. How do you become oblivious to the plight of others whose shoes you once wore?

I would love to be remembered as *Umm Masaakin (the mother of the needy)* amongst other good things. Umm Masaakin not because I am wealthy but because I care enough to want to make the world a better place to live for those less fortunate than myself. This love to share food, love and hope with others gave birth to the **Siddiqah Street Kitchen** (a project I pioneered under Siddiqah Primo Foundation).

Siddiqah Street Kitchen is a mobile food kitchen that caters to the less privileged in their neighbourhoods irrespective of their gender, ethnicity or religion. When thoughts about the project first came to me, I wondered how I was going to raise the funds needed to sustain it. I hoped it would be accepted as a humanitarian project but more importantly as a sadaqatu jaariyah project in the sight of the Most High. I didn't plan for it to blow up so quickly however when we leave our plans in His Hands, He suffices us. I seek no profit from it except making the world a better place one plate and community at a time while bringing hope to others through the project. If you've ever been in a fix expecting a miracle then you'd understand how hope is born through the project.

Imagine you are walking on a hot sunny day with no money in your pocket and no idea of where the next meal will come from. You become exhausted having walked quite a distance, you get to a stop with a seat and you sit to rest your head on the neck of the seat. Someone walks over to where you are seated, calls out to you and hands you food and water with a smile. You do not know this person yet your life is saved as a result of their kindness. This is almost like walking in a desert in search of water and suddenly you come across a well and Alas! It's full with water.

Can you imagine the joy of Hajar (alayha salam) when she came back to her crying child, Ismail (alayhi salam) and found water gushing from beneath his feet? What does her story do to you? How about you being a source of hope to others? This is one of the things I always hoped to achieve with the Street Kitchen project.

I know what hunger is- 1 have tasted it in its realest form. Although I grew up in comfort, life happened. I went through a divorce and the tide changed quite suddenly and unexpectedly. I was presented with the choice of going for something haram (forbidden) or staying hungry. I chose hunger. I could have hidden under the umbrella of darur (that it was permissible in dire times) right? However, if I did, I would not be able to live with the shame, how do I face my Lord when I know 1 participated in an act He explicitly forbade.

I had just invested my last money in a certain business only to find out it had haram elements to a large percentage, I couldn't do anything about it. I had to forfeit the money because earning the pleasure of my Lord was more important than the threat of hunger that appeared imminent. Yorubas (a native tribe in South West Nigeria) would say;

"awe baa awe nile"

meaning

**"there was fasting even before the
month of fasting arrived."**

This quote had become my reality; I would walk a far distance knowing I either used the money I had to take a bus home or buy myself a meal. During those days, whenever my heart wanted to cave, I'd reassure myself saying,

'Aishah, you'd get through this, In Shaa Allah'.

Alhamdulilaah for the blessings of being able to motivate myself through self-talk. I got through it with the help of Ar-Razaq.

**"Verily with hardship comes ease"
(Q 94 vs 1)**

**"Whoever fears Allah,
He will make a way from Him from places
he never even imagined"
(Q 65 vs 2)**

This helped strengthen the Siddiqah dream in my heart. The Siddiqah idea had been born however I was still fine-tuning things so I made use of my pain and supplicated to Allah for its success. I promised myself that I would do everything in my power to bring ease to others if and when Allah granted me success and ease.

"there is no success except with
the help of Allah"
(Q11 vs 88)
(wa maa tawfeeki illa billaah)

Every time we set out for a street kitchen project; every time I have food in abundance; every time I am presented with the opportunity to bring hope to people, I jump at it sometimes over-burdening myself in the process. I stay hopeful that Al-Wahhab would make a way for me to reach ease for He never fails in His promises.

Each and every one of us have tasks Allah has assigned for us, sometimes we have similar assignments so we have to work collaboratively however we all have our given tasks. Even people with different disabilities and life challenges have a part to play for we have all been placed on this earth for a reason. I can only be passionate about my calling. I might not understand what yours is however I have no right to judge you or look down at you because I appear to be in a role of higher authority just as you have no right to judge me for being different from you.

What have you been called here for? What have you been gifted with to help you stay in the minds and hearts of people? What role would you like to fit into that would make it easy for you to contribute your quota to making the world a better place?

A dear sister once reflected on the importance of a doorman in her firm. Even though it may be categorised as a low-level job, his importance was noticed on the day he was absent from work. He opens the door to the building with a smile and acts as a gatekeeper to ensure only staff and clients access the building and alerts security if suspicious characters are lurking around. You see, we all have our roles to play.

Do you know the story of the battle of Uhud? What did we

learn from the archers that were told to guard the back end of the battle field on the side of the Muslims? When the archers saw the battle going in favour of the Muslims, they left their spot and went against the orders of the Nabiy (sallallaahu alayhi wassalam) who had told them not to move from their spot until they were told otherwise. In the end, many Muslims were killed in that battle. In hindsight perhaps if they had realised that their role in that battle was as important as the role of the soldiers in the forefront of the battlefield, they would have stuck to their posts.

What is the essence of our existence on earth if we leave without making an impact that will live on long after we are dead? What is the purpose of our time here if we do not spend it securing for ourselves the best abode in the hereafter?

One of the most beautiful names given to Muslim boys is Bilal. Bilal ibn Rabah (RadiyAllahu anhu) was the Muadhin of the Nabiy (sallallahu alayhi wassalam). He was a man who looked beyond his low status at the time Islam came to Makkah and chose excellence over cowardice. He had every excuse to have stayed away from being a torchbearer of this Ummah but he chose wisely. Colour, pain and lack of class did not stop him from showing admirable character that has earned him the love and respect of many and most importantly -the pleasure of Allah TabarakAllah.

Every day the sun comes up, every day we are able to open our eyes to behold the beautiful sky thus signifying our existence here, we are given another opportunity to live purposefully whilst making the world around us easier on others.

When I made the intention to go ahead with the Street Kitchen project, I initially intended to feed about 20 people every month. From 20 people, the target went up to 200. By the time the Siddiqah volunteer team and I set out on the day of the first Street Kitchen, we hoped to feed about 500 people from the funds we had raised for the project. We ended up sharing 981 meals that day! Allaahu Akbar! From 20 meals to 981 meals! Laa hawla walaa quwatta illa billaah.

The Street Kitchen project is now in its third year running and so far, we have been able to rustle up over 35, 000 meals in more than 25 different communities (See appendix). We have been able to achieve this only with the help of Allaah azza wa jaal. When Allaah calls you to do something, all you need to do is show up and He would perfect His work.

Your dreams are valid and achievable. Your life is very important and it ought to be lived with purpose. If and when you decide not to fill the space you've been asked to fill, Allah will raise someone who will do it better with fewer resources. So, what would you like to be remembered for? Live it and dream it having certainty in the fact that if you stay sincere, He would grant you success.

I am far from achieving all I set out to achieve with the Street Kitchen project. Siddiqah is far from reaching its mark. I am a distance away from achieving my life dreams and goals yet we keep striving and pushing because we know we only need to show up. We only need to tie our camel and Allaah would help us achieve as long as we stay sincere.

Honour is a gift from Allah TabarakAllaah and He honours whom He wills. If you were to engage in a deed sincerely for His sake, He will honour you Himself. Decide on what you'd like to be remembered for, work towards it and know that Allaah would bring you all the help you need to make it a reality.

Trials Upon The Path

In striving to make your life memorable, be rest assured that you will be tested.

Allah say;

*"Do you think you'd be left because
you say,"You believe" and not be tested?"*

He also says,

"....And give glad tidings to the patient"

In the years following my resolve of living an exemplary life, I
faced a lot of pain and hardship sometimes to the point where
I wondered if Allah had denied my request. However, I have
come to learn that His delays are not denials. I am still going
through pain and tough times yet I have chosen to stay on the
path because I know that if I stay patient`, I would get the
ultimate goal I seek -the pleasure of my Lord Most Kind.

The high achievers amongst the people of the past went
through a lot of hardship. Allah mentions this to us in the
Qur'an where He says,

*"Or think you that you will enter Paradise
without such (trials) as came to those who passed
away before you? They were afflicted with severe poverty
and ailments and were so shaken that even the Messenger
and those who believed along with him said,"When
(Will come) the Help of Allah?" Yes! Certainly,
the Help of Allah is near"*
(Q 2 vs 214)

The companions of the Nabiy (sallallaahu alayhi wassalam)
were at their tethers end and almost losing hope. When in a
similar situation along your path to achieving, remember that
help and hope arrive just when it appears that you're about to
break.

Everyone wants to be honoured and amazing. Everyone
would love to live worthy lives yet how many are ready to put
in the work? Sometimes your pain and heartbreak would come

from the people you are trying to benefit; it would come from those supposed to support you. Sometimes the pain would be closer home; from family. It is usually more painful and frustrating when it comes from these quarters. For some, the biggest obstacle in their path to living purposeful lives is their spouse!

For some, it's their parents while for some others it's their children. Can you imagine the pain of Prophet Nuh (alayhi salam) when his son perished along with the wrongdoers? Can you imagine the sadness of Lut (alayhi salam) when his wife disobeyed? Can you imagine how Ibrahim (alayhi salam) felt when his father seemed to be one of his arc enemies in the fight against kufr? Can you imagine how the Nabiy (sallallaahu alayhi wassalam) felt when he was prosecuted by his own clan?

The opposition to achieving your dreams should not deter you from achieving your dreams of leaving your mark in history. It should not deter you from achieving the success. One of my favourite quotes of all times says,

"The future belongs to those who believe
in the beauty of their dreams"
-Eleanor Roosevelt

This was one of my first guiding words before I came across the hadith I shared earlier in this chapter.

Do you believe in your dreams?
Do you believe you can achieve them?
Do you believe you have been called for a higher purpose?

Put in the work, trust in God to help you
achieve success because there is no success
except with His Help.

There would be times you'd work hard and pray even harder yet face hardship, that shouldn't deter you. One of the aspects

58

of my life that has caused me great pain is marriage. I grew up in a secure family and for as long as I can remember I had always wanted to recreate something even better than that so imagine my pain when divorce came along to shatter those carefully planned dreams.

It felt like I was being dealt a blow below the belt; I wondered if my prayers were answered. It distracted me for some time but I was reminded of the pain and hardship of those who came before who strove to be relevant. I decided there and then to always find a way to make my way back to the path leading towards my dreams.

It will get really stormy sometimes, hold on to the Lord of the storm and you will get through it. This world has its highs and lows. Just as you'd not quit travelling because the road got rather bumpy, stay focused on the goal while moving towards it or die trying to reach it. What does it profit you to come to this world and leave with a full tank just because you were too scared? Living in fear of what pain lies behind an achievement would not prevent time from passing so make every second you have left count. Remember, when it's your turn to answer the last call, there will be no extra check-out time.

I would love to be remembered as someone who walked her talk defying all odds whilst seeking the pleasure of Allaah TabarakAllah.

What will you be remembered for?

Reflections

○As we journey through life, we would face hardships and pain that would shake us to our very core -hold on tight.

○What is the worth of your life if you do not live it in a way that makes you relevant, dead or alive?

○True relevance is seen after we depart; would your absence be felt?

○Sometimes our setbacks would come from those supposed to have our back -you are not alone as others before you suffered a similar fate yet they endured and still made their mark.

○Believe in yourself, go ahead and work towards achieving them while trusting in God to grant you success.

Verily the life of this world is filled
with highs and lows; hills and mountains.
It gets hot and cold too. The true worth
of a person's life is not in how much he
accumulated of wealth but in how
impactful he lived his life.

"And give glad tidings to the patient"
Q2 vs 155

5.
Get
Ready!

Exiting the life of this world with all its ups and downs is not an issue, the real problem is in what lies in wait after the exit.

*Is your exit a beautiful exit to bliss
and rest or is it to eternal pain and anguish?*

*Is your grave from the gardens of Jannah
or is it filled with snakes and dreadful looking
creatures as companions?*

Everyone wants to end up with a good end but how many are willingly putting in the work that would get them their intended results? Whenever I think of death, what lingers in my mind is this – in the life of this world, we run back to Allaah whenever the going gets tough and it can get really ugly sometimes. In most of these earthly trials, it's either trouble brought on by a fellow being or a situation you have no doubt can be changed with Allaah's help and intervention. Now my question is,

"Who do you run to when the One punishing you is Allaah?!

Who can rescue you from the trials and tribulations of the grave when the One calling you to account is Ash-Shedidul Iqab?

Who do you turn to for mercy when you have been denied mercy by Ar-Rahman?"

Thoughts such as these stop me in my tracks when I seem to

be going on a tangent away from that which I am supposed to do. His Mercy is abundant yet His punishment is very severe. The wise one is he who looks forward to being encompassed in His Mercy and works towards it.

From His Mercy is that he has gifted us many different ways to earn His pleasure and come towards His ultimate gift (Jannah), wouldn't you take heed? Wouldn't you like to be one of those who enjoys the unlimited and unimaginable pleasures of that beautiful place? A place that NO eyes have seen and the mind cannot even comprehend or conjure up the image of beauty awaiting us.

I would love to be there with my loved ones. I would love for you to be there as well so I invite you to start getting ready to disembark from this ship of life so we are not caught unaware. I invite you to discipline your soul so it doesn't get you into trouble with Al-Jabbar for on that day no one would be dealt with unjustly. Everyone would be given the reward for their actions and/or inactions in full.

A woman of wisdom once said to me,

"Allaah does not expect from us perfection so He did not create us to be perfect in character else our punishment would have been instantaneous. He created us to strive to be the best that we can be. He left with us His forgiveness and mercy that we might strive to excel bearing in mind that we can seek His forgiveness when we fall short of His guidance".

In preparing for our exit, here are some deeds you can engage in that would help us as we transition into eternal life.

Sadaqatu Jaariyah -*Continuous Charity*

What continuous charitable act can you engage in that would grant you lots of goodness long after you've departed?

○**You may plant trees in an area where there is a**

scarcity; for everyone that passes by it and benefits from its shade, you get rewarded.

○There is a scarcity of clean water in many places around the world; have you considered banding together with family and friends to build a well or create a way for those communities to have access to clean drinking water?

○It could be that you participate in the rehabilitation of certain roads making life easier for those who ply that road.

○**Providing food security to impoverished or low-income areas around you?**

○**You could also take part in a project ensuring there is a suitable graveyard to bury Muslims in your locality.**

○**Sponsoring a less privileged upright Muslim for hajj. Imagine the reward for every tawaf the pilgrim makes?**

These are just a few suggestions; there are countless ways in which you can contribute towards a continuous charitable project. You don't have to be the one initiating the project because it may be difficult to figure out the logistics of these projects. However, there are many organisations and in some cases individuals who identify these projects and ask for funds from the public. You can contribute meaningfully and positively towards laudable projects being set up around you. Most times your man power support goes a long way in making a difference. For example, not everyone had money to contribute towards the feeding done through Siddiqah, but they were able to contribute in other ways. Some people helped in cooking, packing, distributing the food, video coverage of the event and some who owned vehicles helped to transport us to the various locations.

Always ensure that whenever you get involved in these

projects, you do so sincerely seeking the pleasure of your Lord so you get your rewards in full. It is easy to become derailed and overcome by people's admiration and accolades. Do not abandon the good act because of this, simply re-set your intentions and continue it to the end.

Often times, people find it difficult to trust projects set up by other people outside their circle of friends. I would suggest that due diligence be carried out to ascertain the authenticity of the project and if you still do not feel comfortable contributing your quota in cash and/or kind, support these projects with your prayers.

"Verily, continuous charity
is from the deeds beloved to Allaah
which would bring you peace in your graves"

Benefiting Others With Relevant Knowledge

From the deeds most beloved to Allaah TabarakAllah is dispersing knowledge that is of great benefit to the people and this is not limited to knowledge about the religion. Imagine sharing the knowledge of how to stay healthy with others thus assisting them stay fit for the worship of Allah? It could be that you have information on how to strengthen one's mind thus helping them get through tough times easily. You might have the knowledge of how to cook healthy and tasty meals which help people bring joy to their families and loved ones.

Whenever I am blessed with the opportunity to speak to people either during a training or during a talk, I often say, God has not created anyone except that He has blessed them with a gift that would help them excel. What gift do you have that is currently sitting on the shelf? We would not all be scholars; we are not all orators and we are not all adept at writing however we can contribute our quota to supporting those blessed with the skills thus sharing in the reward of spreading beneficial knowledge. Strive to benefit others from that which you know of knowledge in a way that makes them live better. Share knowledge at the level and extent to which you know it.

With advancement in technology, it has become even easier to share things of benefit. Rather than spend your every waking moment chasing after irrelevant news of what is happening in the lives of others, perhaps you can take out time to share from that which you know that is of benefit. It could be in short messages; it could be in long articles. Whichever way works for you is fine as long as you ensure you do not die with all that good stuff buried inside of you as that would be a great injustice to yourself and humanity.

Attachment To The Qur'an

Human beings are an interesting set of Allah's creation. Imagine a person gets a job; part of his work tools and needs include a black book which contains all the rules and information that would help him get to the top of the ladder quickly. How do you think he'd relate with this book? He'd probably keep this book close to his heart studying it and striving to live by its rules whenever he is at work.

Why then are we so complacent and distant from the 'black book of life' -the Qur'an? A book Allah says is; hudan lilmutaqeen -a guide for people who fear Him much.

The guide has all we need to make our way through this world successfully. It has warnings, advice, stories, parables, inspirational words and all we need as humans to live well in this world yet many of us have it in our homes only as evidence to the fact that we are Muslims. Really? Is that all its supposed to be for? We neither read it nor interact with its verses. We'd rather spend time laying away in front of the TV set than sit with it for some time to gain guidance. We leave it to gather dust on our shelves giving the excuse that we are really busy. Sadly, some of us only remember it when the month of Ramadhan approaches and can't wait to drop it the moment the month ends.

The successful ones are those who attach themselves to its message, ponder over its meaning while seeking Allah's Help from straying away from its teachings. How many of you still remember their times table? You probably still do because of the level of practice and attention you gave it. Spend time with the Qur'an just as you did with the times table. Read it, memorise it and live by its teachings. We are all on the path towards our Lord and He knows best how we'd travel towards Him. Take from His guidance and heed His words knowing that by doing this we would be preparing for a blissful meeting with Him (azza wa jaal).

Raise Righteous Children

From those actions that draws a person closer to the pleasure of Allah and grants one goodness in the grave are righteous offspring.
I listened to a lecture by *Sr Zohra Sarwari* where she said,

"Do not kill your children."

Naturally, you'd be taken aback by that statement. No sane parent would want to kill their children. But what she was telling us was;

"Do not kill your children by spoiling them."

That day I appreciated my parents more as there was no opportunity to get spoilt with the way we were raised.

Many parents now have a different philosophy from how we

were raised. "Spare the rod and spoil the child." I do not approve of child abuse; however, I agree that children need to be disciplined. Our children need to learn to play outdoors and communicate and interact with us and each other without the technology gadgets. Many parents are busy making money and this takes them away from their children more than they would like and in order to fill the void, they over-compensate by making sure the children do not lack anything or are not denied anything no matter the expense.

We only need to relate with our children with taqwa while supplicating for them and about them thus making our love for them shine through. I was raised in a home where discipline was a given and it hasn't stopped me from loving or supplicating for my parents. I did disagree with certain aspects of the training; however, I have come to appreciate them more since becoming a parent. I do not believe in powdering the truth especially where the upbringing of a child is on the table.

I do not spare my children when they deserve to be scolded just as I do not hesitate to tell them and show them I love them dearly. It's all about striking a balance. The greatest disservice you can do to your children is to allow them all liberties just because you don't want to see them cry or unhappy. Children see through our actions and they know when an act is out of love and otherwise. It might take some time for them to acknowledge it; however, they will come to love and thank you in the end.

Relate with them with the fear of God; treat them with as much love and kindness as you possibly can while instilling in them God consciousness and good manners. You'd be the better for it. Raising righteous children benefits you not only while you are here but also in your grave.

Our Lord grant us spouses and offspring that are the coolness to our eyes and make them arise from amongst them leaders of the people of righteousness. Aamiyn.

Bringing Ease To Others

We live in times where people are concerned more about receiving than about giving. Even those who have want to take some more. It is a competition for whose garden is the biggest. We forget that life is not all about the size of our garden but more about the richness of the soil in that garden. How about you defy the norm and strive to be different in a way that counts.

You do not have to be rich or comfortable to bring ease to others around you, you only need to care. Wouldn't it be nice to get help from those who have and give to the have-nots? Can you imagine the joy you'd spread to the hearts of those you bring ease to? Sometimes you enjoy good fortune without realising you are benefiting from the supplication of one whose life you changed.

Bringing ease to others isn't always in material things, it could be immaterial as well. Sometime last year, I met a sister whose family was going through a rough patch. She had been referred to me by someone who had worked with me. The sister who referred her felt she could benefit from the work we do at Siddiqah. Unfortunately, she came at a time when funds were really low and we had a lot of pending cases. I took a glance at her and the child she came with and I was really sad I couldn't offer as much help as I would have loved. Just then, Allah guided me to words which I said to her by way of motivating her to not despair. I reminded her of the love of Allah and that He was not unaware of her travails and He would send help soon. I spoke to her till I could see her shoulders relax and her face lightened up a bit. I gave her my out of office number and gave her the go ahead to reach out to me anytime she felt the need to and I could see her leave happier than when she arrived. I was able to send her off with a little stipend to relieve their burden at least for that day.

Some days later, I received a message from her saying I didn't know what I did for her however Allah knows and he'd reward me. She went on to say; "I was going to commit suicide that day I came around; my family had forsaken me and I felt all alone. Your words gave me hope."At first, I thought I had misread the message so I reread it again and this time I couldn't help myself; I got very emotional. As tears streamed down my face, I kept supplicating to Allah to make a way out for Siddiqah (The NGO I run). I asked that He make my team and I a means of bringing smiles to many families, this sister's family inclusive.

If you've never had it tough, you may never be able to understand how low a person gets to the point of hopelessness. We are not the same in strength. Some are stronger than others hence our ability to withstand hardship varies. Never compare your trial to someone else's. Be a source of hope for people and not a dark cloud that sucks out the beauty in their sky. Yes, some people exaggerate their problems and milk the situation. There are still many genuine cases out there so be kind. Imagine how fortunate you'd be if you are able to sprinkle these acts of kindness everywhere you go. It would add colour to your world and bring ease to your life in the hereafter.

Make your presence count as much as you can.
Leave people in a better situation than you meet them
and if you're unable to do this do not make their
life any harder than it already is.

Reflections

◦*Engage in deeds that would add colour to your life*

in the hereafter.

◦ *Stay focused on your preparations for the last call so you do not end up a loser*

◦ *Trust in Allah to bless your efforts and make your sojourn easy.*

*And in the end, all praises to
the One who accepts all good and
forgives us, for to Him is our
final return.*

Epilogue

In this book, I have shared with you my reflections and thoughts on death and how it has impacted upon my life and actions. Below are accounts of real people with death either as a close call, or as a result of losing a loved one either after an extended period of illness or suddenly.

It is my hope that these interviews would give context to the sharing and help you take action in living intently and purposefully. The section after the interviews contains advice on what to do if you are around someone who is about to pass away or if you are invited to help with the process of losing a loved one or sending off another Muslim who has departed this world.

I hope you find the notes in here beneficial and helpful.

BaarakAllahu Feekum.

A Close Call

Interview with Umm Amatullaah abbreviated as UA

AA: As salamu alaykum sis

UA: Wa alaykumu salam warahmatullaah wabarakatuh sis

AA: How are you doing today?

UA: Alhamdulilaah

AA: Thank you for agreeing to share with us. I am indeed humbled and grateful.

UA: Smiles. Alhamdulillaah

AA: WHAT were some of your dreams and goals growing up? Are you close to achieving them? How near or far are you?

UA: Well, growing up I wanted to care for people. So (I) was tilted towards the medical profession. Coming from a third world country, I have seen my fair share of avoidable deaths and I wanted to be a part of those reducing the burden. I dreamt of owning a clinic that would have 2 sections; a section for those who could pay and one for those who couldn't afford treatment. I planned to take out part of the profit from the paying side to help the poor.
I am yet to achieve this dream however I am working towards it. I would say, I am far from achieving my goals however I am hopeful that Allah would grant me success.

AA: I understand you had a near death experience. How was it like for you? What was going through your mind whilst it was going on?

UA: Hmmm. Alhamdulillaah in all circumstances. Yes, I did have a near death experience. I honestly thought the end had come. SubhaanAllaah and I was pretty scared of what was to come after. I kept thinking is this really it, yaa Rabb. I had been involved in an almost fatal domestic accident. It was a good thing I was not home alone the day it happened else I'd probably not be able to share this today. I was very scared of what the hereafter held for me; I was scared of what was going to happen to my child as I had a lot I had not been able to share with her for she was still quite little then. I had my life flash before me and I just resigned my fate to whatever Allaah gave to me.

When I remembered that my last deed before the accident occurred was a deed in which I had made sajdah to Allaah, I relaxed a bit and just looked to Him for Mercy.

AA: What changed in how you spent your days following the incident?

UA: I started to re-evaluate my life and started doing somethings I had left off because I was unsure of how it'd be accepted. Many of us live in fear holding back because we don't want people to talk. People talk when you act and they talk when you don't act so how about you act? I became almost completely unfazed by the opinions of people and worked more on purifying my intention and going for what I wanted to achieve. Alhamdulillaah it has helped me move mountains I never thought I could move

AA: What advice do you have for us?

UA: Live in the moment and do a lot of good while you still can. Life ends in a flash. Every time I think back to that day, I am reminded that I have been given another opportunity to better myself and I shouldn't blow it.

Not everyone escapes from the kind of accident I survived, so prepare yourself for death every single day knowing that one of those days would surely be your last.

AA: SubhaanAllaah. Thank you for your words of wisdom.

UA: You are welcome. Jazaakillaahu khayran for giving me the opportunity to share.

AA: Aamiyn wa antum fa jazaakAllaahu khayran

Interview With Those
Who Lost A Loved One

Umm Anas was informed of the death of her father one morning around the time for the pre-dawn prayers. Below is an interview with her and her reflections as a result of the loss.

Interview excerpts from Umm Anas

AA: As salamu alaykum

Umm Anas: Wa alaykum salaam Warahmatullaah wabarakatuhu

AA: How are you doing today?

Umm Anas: Not bereft of Allaah's mercies, Alhamdulillaah Katheeran

AA: Thank you for agreeing to share with us. I am indeed humbled and grateful.

AA: Before your loss, what were your thoughts about death? Was it something you reflected upon?

Umm Anas: I knew death would come unannounced and unexpected. Yes, I used to reflect on death a lot because I had lost friends unexpectedly but I think the reality of it happening to someone I truly loved had not dawned on me

AA: What went through your mind when you heard the news?

Umm Anas: I actually didn't know how to react, then I started hoping in Allah for a miracle that it would be a scare and that Allah will restore his soul back to us.

AA: How did you feel when you saw the body of your loved one?

Umm Anas: Blank and scared and I started thinking about the grave and summoned the courage to make dua'a as much as I could.

AA: What lessons did you draw from their departure?

Umm Anas: I could be next; what am I preparing for my akhirah? Are my current actions/deeds enough to make me enter Jannaah?

AA: How has it impacted upon your life?

Umm Anas: To be a better Muslim and obey the commandments of Allah and worship Him as if I see Him. I honestly don't want to have any regrets on Yaomul Hisaab. May Allah help me

AA: What advice do you have to share with others based on this experience?

Umm Anas: Never ever joke with what Allah has commanded you to do, give Allah His rights, worship Him sincerely and repent. No one is promised the next second, minute or hour. My dad's friend passed on the day of Eid; he left his home to felicitate with his friend and never made it back. Death is behind you; how will you have fared when it catches up with you?

Interview with Umm Muhammad

AA: As salamu alaykum sis

UM: Wa alaykumu salam warahmatullaah wabarakatuh sis

AA: How are you doing today?

UM: Alhamdulilaah, I'm good

AA: Thank you for agreeing to share with us. I am indeed

humbled and grateful.

UM: No problem at all sis. Alhamdulillaah.

AA: Before your loss, what were your thoughts about death? Was it something you reflected upon?

UM: Thank you for having me share here. Death seemed so final so I sort of didn't like to dwell on it whenever it crossed my mind. I reflected on it occasionally. The thought of never seeing the person again for a very long time seemed so scary. It's the reality though.

AA: What went through your mind when you heard the news of your loss?

UM: I was thrown off. I was shocked. Though he was old, I just wasn't prepared for his exit. No one is ever prepared to hear they have lost a dear one.

AA: How did you feel when you saw the body of your loved one?

UM: I just kept thinking; this is really final. Unfortunately, I didn't get to see the face before he was taken away for washing and shrouding. All I had left was the memory of him and what his face looked like.

AA: What lesson(s) did you draw from the departure?

UM: I learnt that it was important to show one's loved ones how much you care and cherish them while you have time together. Treat every interaction as if it's a goodbye for the time would come when it would really be a goodbye.

AA: How has it impacted upon your life?

UM: It has made me become more conscious of my practice of the Deen. Helped me stop giving excuses.

AA: What do you wish for people to know?

UM: it is important that people know that our time here is meant to be cherished and appreciated. Every moment we are able to spend with those we care about should be spent wisely. I wish I had another opportunity to sit and speak to him; however, that is not going to happen.

Interview from Umm Saud

AA: As salamu alaykum

UMM SAUD: Waalaekum Salam waramatulah wabarakatuh

AA: How are you doing today?

UMM SAUD: Alhamdullilah, I am very well, thank you.

AA: Thank you for agreeing to share with us. I am indeed humbled and grateful.

UMM SAUD: It's my pleasure.

AA: Before your loss, what were your thoughts about death? Was it something you reflected upon?

UMM SAUD: Not at all. I was a teenager; I had never really dwelled on death. Don't get me wrong, as a child I knew about heaven and hell, living and dying but I had never truly thought about it in depth.

AA: What went through your mind when you heard the news?

UMM SAUD: To be honest nothing really, my body and mind just shut down.

AA: How did you feel when you saw the body of your loved one?

UMM SAUD: Shocked, It didn't fully register until she was being lowered in the grave .

AA: What lessons did you draw from their departure?

UMM SAUD: Hmm, first of all to truly fear and worship Allah like every day is your last because for my mum, her death was a ricochet of events. She was fasting that day and we had just finished our iftar, getting ready for maghrib when she collapsed and had her first seizure. That was the last time she ever fasted and stood in prayer. So, you see, death can happen at any time. What do you want your last moments to be? That's the question I constantly ask myself.
Secondly, be kind to anyone and everyone. My mother was a nurse in general hospital, Till this day, you know how nearly impossible it is to see a doctor in general hospital however anytime I go people recognise my mother's name and make sure I am first in line to see a doctor.
And lastly, to love and be loved. My mother loved her family wholeheartedly and made sure she did everything she could to make us morally upright and religious. That is one important lesson I am trying to incorporate in my little family, May Allah make it easy.

AA: How has it impacted upon your life?

UMM SAUD: For one, I don't take good health for granted. I try to be as active as I can and be present for my kids because let's face facts, death is inevitable on us all. It's the memories that we will have once our loved ones are gone. I don't want my kids to remember that I cooked and cleaned, but I was there and held their hands through every high and low in their lives.

AA: What advice do you have to share with others based on this experience?

UMM SAUD: My biggest regret is I was attempting to be a rebellious teenager and having a sick mum meant I had to grow up fast and while my friends were out playing and living life, I was cooking and cleaning and I didn't want to admit it then but I low-key resented it. I didn't understand the gravity of my mum's illness and I don't think I told her enough how much I loved my mum. If you have your loved ones, let them know it. There's nothing corny about saying "I love you". You really don't have to be wait till a birthday or an anniversary.

What To Do When Someone Dies

We have been going through reflections about death and what to expect; what then should you do when a loved one passes away or you are around a place when a Muslim answers the last call? Below are some things you can do in no particular order.

It is sunnah to do the following when a person is dying and eventually dies:

○**Guide the dying person to say;**

> "*La ilaaha illaa-Allaah*" *(there is no deity worthy of worship except Allah).*

Evidence:

It is narrated on the authority of Abu Sa'id al-Khudri that the Prophet, (sallallahu alayhi wassalam) said:

> "*Prompt your dying people to say:*
> '*La ilaaha illaa-Allah*'."

(Muslim, Abu Daw'ud, Tirmidhi)

Another report on the authority of Mu'adh ibn Jabal states that the Messenger of Allah, peace be upon him, said;

"He whose last words are 'La ilaaha illaa-Allah' shall enter Paradise."

(Narrated by Abu Daw'ud; Al-Hakim considers it a sound hadith)

This prompting at the point of death is necessary when the dying person is unable to utter the shahadah (testimony of faith). If on the other hand the dying person is able to utter these words then there is no need for prompting. Such advice is useful in cases of persons who are in possession of their faculties of reason and speech.

○**Lay the dying person so that the qibla is on his right side.**
Evidence:

It is recorded that Abu Qatadah said:

"Upon arrival in Madinah, the Prophet, (sallallahu alayhi wassalam), enquired about a person called al-Bara ibn Ma'rur. The people told the Prophet, (sallallahu alayhi wassalam), that he had died, and had willed one-third of his property to the Prophet(sallallahu alayhi wassalam) and that his face be turned toward the Ka'bah at the time of his death.

Hearing this, the Prophet, (sallallahu alayhi wassalam), said:

'He has been true to his innate nature.
I return the one-third of his property to his children.'

Then the Prophet, (sallallahu alayhi wassalam), left and offered a prayer for him and prayed, saying:

'O Allah! Forgive him, have mercy on him,
and cause him to enter Your Paradise. Indeed,
you have accepted this prayer'."

(Narrated by Al-Baihaqi and Al-Hakim, who observes: "I know of no hadith, other than this one, with regard to turning the face of a dying person toward Ka'bah.")

○**Close the eyes of the deceased.**
Evidence:

It is narrated by Muslim that the Prophet,
(sallallahu alayhi wassalam), went to visit Abu Salmah.
He saw that his eyes were wide open and blank with
the stare of death. So, the Prophet, (sallallahu
alayhi wassalam), closed his eyes and said:

*"Verily, when a soul is seized,
the eyesight follows it."*

○**Cover the deceased**
Evidence:

Aaishah (radiyAllahu anha) said:

"When the Messenger of Allah (sallallahu alayhi wassalam)
died, he was covered with a piece of cloth that had some
designs on it."

This is reported by Bukhari and Muslim.

The objective here is clearly to safeguard the respect and dignity
of the deceased in death against prying eyes and against the
exposure of his or her body to the idle curiosity of those
looking for changes in its physical condition and features.

○**Prepare the body for burial without delay, as soon as the
death has been confirmed (by a qualified physician or the
like).**

○**The near relatives or associates of the deceased should
wash, wrap, and arrange for the burial of the body.**
Evidence:

This is based on a report, recorded by
Abu Daw'ud from al-Husayn ibn Wujuh

that when Talhah ibn al-Bara fell ill, the Prophet,
(sallallahu alayhi wassalam), said:

*"I see that Talhah is on the verge of death.
Inform me about him (when he passes away) and
make immediate preparations for his burial,
for a Muslim's remains should not be left long
with his family after his death."*

○**Hasten to settle the debt of the deceased.**
Evidence:

Ahmad, Ibn Majah, and Tirmidhi have recorded
a hadith on the authority of Abu Hurairah that the
Messenger of Allah (sallallahu alayhi wassalam) said:

*"A believer's soul remains in suspense
until all his debts are paid off."*

Tirmidhi considers this a sound hadith.

Al-Bukhari records on the authority
of Abu Hurayrah that the Prophet,
peace be upon him, said:

*"If anyone takes other people's money with
the intention to repay it and then he or she should
die without settling the debt, Allah will pay the debt
on his behalf. And if anyone takes money or property
(of others) with the intention of destroying it,
Allah will destroy him."*

Another hadith recorded by Ahmad,
Abu Nu'aym, Al-Bazzar, and At-Tabarani from
the Prophet, (sallallahu alayhi wassalam), says:

"The debtor will be summoned before Allah
on the Day of Judgement.
Then Allah will ask him:

*'O Son of Adam! Why did you incur debt
and infringe on others ' rights?'*

The man would reply:

*'My Lord! You know I took it, but I neither
abused nor lost it. It was stolen or burned in a fire
or lost its value.'*

Allah, the Almighty and Exalted, will say:

*'My slave has told the truth, and I am more entitled
(than anyone else) to settle his debt.*

Then Allah will issue a command and something
will be placed on his scales causing his good deeds
to outweigh his bad ones. And so, by Allah's Grace,
he will enter Paradise'."

◦**Show kindness to the family the deceased left behind**
Evidence:

Abdullah ibn Ja'far reported
that the Messenger of Allah,
(sallallahu alayhi wassalam), said:

*"Prepare some food for the family of Ja'far,
for what has befallen them is keeping
them preoccupied."*

This is narrated by Abu Daw'ud, Ibn Majah and Tirmidhi,
who grades it as a sound hadith.

◦**Reflect over this death and prepare for your own demise
as well by getting your shroud (kaftan).**
Evidence:

Imam Ahmad (Rahimahullaah
was reported to have said:

*"There is nothing wrong if a person purchases
a site for his burial and makes a will to the effect
that he is to be buried there. 'Uthman, 'Aishah,
and 'Umar ibn Abd al-'Aziz, all did so."*

Reporting on the authority of Sahl, Imam Bukhari
(Rahimahullaah) says:

"A woman came to the Prophet,
(sallallahu alayhi wassalam), with a woven piece
of cloth that had two seams on its edges.
She said:

'I wove it with my own hands in order to wear it.'

The Prophet, peace be upon him, took it
because he needed it. He wrapped it around his
waist so that it covered the lower half of his body,
and he came toward us. A man praised it, saying:

*'This is a very nice cloth! Why don't you
give it to me to wear?'*

Some of the people present there reproached
the man for they knew that the Prophet needed
that cloth and that he never denied anyone's request.
The man replied:

*'By Allah, I asked him for it not to wear it,
but to save it and use it as my kaftan'."*

Sahl continues:

*"And (later when he died) that same piece of
cloth was used as his kaftan."*

NB: Siddiqah DeenHub has put together the **Janaazah pack** which is a pack that contains all you need to use for the washing and shrouding of the deceased. The DeenHub also organises Janazaah Workshops to educate muslims on how to proceed with this.

For enquiries, send an email to info@siddiqahdeenhub.com

Resources

You have engaged with the contents in this book and the contents might have challenged you and pushed you to want to level-UP. As such, I would like to support you further towards healing, growth and impact.

PEEL THE LAYERS JOURNAL

This is a self-discovery journal that has quotes, question prompts and affirmations to make you feel empowered.

PEEL THE LAYERS WORKSHOP AND SELF PACED COURSE

This is a self-discovery course that helps you dig deep into your core to reveal what is on the inside. It is a course that helps you understand who you are, why you react to certain things the way you do and why you connect to certain people in a certain way, all based on your personality. It is a deep dive into who you are. Those who have completed the course have graduated from it feeling empowered with the knowledge to go and be amazing. It is conducted as a 2-day workshop as well as a self-paced online course.

SELF DISCOVERY CARDS

As you embark on your self-discovery journey, there would be moments where you need to be reminded of why you should hold still and follow through; these cards are the companion you need for those kinds of days. Beautifully designed and pocket friendly.

SELF WORTH AFFIRMATION CARDS

These are a set of affirmation cards that would help you boost your morale at those moments you feel low. They are easy to carry around cards.

THE WHITE ELEPHANT MASTERMIND

This is a seminar where we own up to emotions that are not serving us so we can finally release them and grow past them. Since tests have beauty in them, our work with you is centred around helping you embrace the pain so it no longer holds you back.

THURSDAY TREATS

This is my podcast series where I talk about healing, growth, impact and related issues. New episodes drop on Thursdays. Guests are invited now and then to discuss different topics. Overall, we support your growth journey with audio talks to help you stay motivated. Check out our podcasts on Soundcloud.

JANAZAH WORKSHOPS

DeenHub is the spirituality arm of Siddiqah and it has conducted a couple of janazah workshops to teach people practical ways of washing and shrouding the dead. There are also Janazah Packs available for purchase which contains all you need to wash and shroud the dead, bi ithnillaah.

SISTERS SPEAK AND SHARE SERIES

This is a show where a number of ladies come together to discuss issues that affect women across the world with focus on women of African descent.

LET THE SUN IN

This is a course on healing that starts you on the path towards forgiveness and growth. The first step towards healing is forgiveness and there are steps that you can take to release negative emotions.

FORGIVE YOURSELF JOURNAL

This is a journal that has been created to support people on their forgiveness and healing journey. There are prompts and affirmations to help you experience healing if you engage with the journal as you ought to.

FORGIVENESS AFFIRMATION CARDS

These are a set of cards that you can easily carry around to aid you on your forgiveness and healing journey. They have been beautifully designed to soothe the eyes and help you experience ease and release.

Charity Work

Siddiqah Foundation is the charitable arm of Siddiqah International which is a personal and community development organisation built to impact the lives of people and communities across the world. Siddiqah Foundation is big on nourishing optimism. We believe a person who is hopeful can achieve anything. The problem is that most people lose hope in themselves and those around them and we are happy to be the support they need to swim through the waters of divorce and widowhood. We also support struggling families so they can get back on their feet. We share our message of love and hope with marginalized communities experiencing extreme poverty and deprivation as well. So far, we have supported more than 100,000 people across more than 35 communities in Nigeria, Africa. We also run health advocacy programmes that help people access the necessary information to help them stay healthy.

We work tirelessly to bring joy and hope to people through our work. Check out www.siddiqahfoundation.org for more information.

About The Author

AISHAH ADAMS also known as "The Mind Doctor" is an NLP-trained transformational speaker, coach, certified counsellor, public health professional and author. As the acclaimed author of The White Elephant, Rise, Irrespective! The Last Call and other self-development tools, she often writes on issues around mental and emotional wellness, health, personal development and topics that impact the lives of women and their families. She is also a Lisa Nichols-trained public speaker and a serial social entrepreneur who is committed to several high impact community development projects.

Aishah Adams is the founder of Siddiqah International and The Support Lounge. The Support Lounge is a transformational coaching, training and therapy hub that helps users heal from pain and foster personal growth. This is a hub where she hosts emotional and mental wellness workshops, runs soft skills training as well as one to one coaching for driven women who are looking to grow out of the rut they are currently in to birth their purpose. She walks women through healing from pain, whilst supporting them to leverage on their pain to birth their purpose. She runs soft skills training ranging from self-discovery to emotional intelligence to resilience building workshops all geared towards helping her tribe grow holistically.

Siddiqah, on the other hand is a personal and community development organization built to impact the lives of people and communities across the world through support and empowerment of stigmatized groups such as widows, divorcees and families experiencing extreme poverty. Over 1,000 families have been supported over the last 8 plus years.

She is also the brain behind My Street Kitchen project which is a project under the Outreach arm of Siddiqah that has catered to over 150,000 people across Nigeria. My Street Kitchen is a monthly outreach to slums that provides food, clothes, soft skills training and hands-on skills acquisition that can be monetized by the poor to improve their standard of living.

Aishah is a social researcher, social skills trainer and community development professional who has strength in Data Processing as well as Crisis Intervention and Disaster Management following her training with University of Minnesota in 2012 during her Masters at the University of Wolverhampton, United Kingdom. She has an attentive ear and an open mind.

If you or your organisation are looking for a passionate speaker to address issues that affect women, disadvantaged people, impactful projects or you are just looking to motivate people to get them to take action, look no further!

Speaking Information

If you would like to invite Aishah to speak at your next event, kindly send an email to speak@aishahadams.com and we will get back to you within 2-3 working days. Alternatively, you can head over to www.aishahadams.com to fill in the speaking engagement form.

If you have a question about the book or coaching or you just want to do something impactful and awesome and you are seeking a passionate speaker to engage with the audience then send us an email at info@aishahadams.co
See you soon!

PLEASE NOTE
A percentage of the royalties from this book goes to Siddiqah, which provides support to families experiencing extreme poverty and stigma. As you get your transformation from this book, you will also be helping people in need find help, *so thank you.*

And in the end, all praise to the Lord of the worlds; I am eternally grateful to Him and I ask that He accepts this from me as a means of seeking His Face

Appendix

Some Projects You Can Support

1. LEND A HAND

This is the tag name for the support and empowerment scheme for Siddiqah Primo Foundation. Siddiqah supports widows, divorcees and struggling families under this scheme. Beneficiaries are supported psychologically, emotionally and sometimes financially when funds are available to help them stabilize. This scheme has supported over 43 families. For more information you can send a mail or text +2348091839097. Alternatively, you can send donations to Siddiqah quoting LAH as reference.

Siddiqah, Stanbic ibtc 0015221192

2. SIDDIQAH STREET KITCHEN PROJECT (SSK)

The Siddiqah Street Kitchen project is in the third year of its activities. It is a mobile food kitchen that caters to the less privileged living in deprived areas in different communities. There is a goal to establish food banks across localities where the hunger index is steep. It runs once every month and is able to provide meals for at least 1000 people per Street Kitchen. For more information about the Street Kitchen project please send a mail to info@siddiqahfoundation.org . You can also call or text +2348175525908

To support the SSK project, please send your donations to Siddiqah, Stanbic ibtc, 0015221192 quoting SSK as reference.

3. SPONSOR A HUJJAJ PROJECT

This project is being run on behalf of a sister who passed away after a long illness. It is intended to raise and finance the hajj trip for the poor, upright Muslims living in Africa. Operations are currently being run from Nigeria. Every year, there is call for people to apply, a test is done and shortlisted candidates are sponsored depending on the funds available for this project. Going for hajj is not a life-threatening problem however it is all some people need to feel fulfilled. Focus is on people with disabilities and the aged who have never been opportune to make the hajj.

4. VOLUNTEER

We always welcome volunteers; they are an integral part of our workforce at Siddiqah. You can volunteer your time for any of the aforementioned projects by sending a mail to aishah.adams12@gmail.com to register your interest and you would be linked with the appropriate personnel.

5. GROW A COMMUNITY

This is the humanitarian crisis and community development project section tag for Siddiqah. Here we sponsor community development projects that impact positively on communities in the areas of education, water supply, road rehabilitation and food security. We have successfully commissioned a couple of projects which has provided water for communities being challenged by it. To support this initiative, you can send donations to Siddiqah quoting GAC

Funds should be sent to Siddiqah, 0015221192, Stanbic ibtc bank.

6. SIDDIQAH RAMADHAN PROJECTS

This harbours two key projects;

Siddiqah Ramadhan Relief Pack and;

Siddiqah Ramadhan Feeding Scheme.

Over the last 5 years Siddiqah Primo Foundation has provided relief to families as well as daily iftar meals for rough sleepers. Over 1000 families have benefited from the relief pack scheme. As at last count, Siddiqah catered to over 20,000 poor indigenes during the last Ramadhan. You can support either of the 2 Ramadhan Projects by sending your donations to the Siddiqah account.

7. EID MEAT DRIVE AND GIFT SHARE

This was a project we kicked off in 2017. It was intended to help families of the less privileged have food to eat and feed their families with during the Eid ul Adha celebration. Here, we distribute Eid Meat Packs to families as well as distribute food packs to the streets for rough sleepers. We also share gifts to the families so they are included in the festivities. No one should have to go hungry during seasons of happiness because they do not have.

Final Thoughts

*Wherever you go, whatever you do,
however you do it,*

Never forget the destroyer of pleasure -death

*Plan for your demise more thoroughly than you'd plan for
your next meal.*

This world is not ours, our stay here is very temporary

*So remember, when the time comes for you to leave there
would be no coming back here.*

*May Allaah take us back to Him when He is most
pleased with us, make our last deeds the best of our deeds
and our graves from the gardens of Jannah.*

*O Allah, make our standing before you easy and grant us
easy entry into Jannatul firdaous.*

Aamiyn.

Printed in Great Britain
by Amazon

74610070R00068